Divorce

MARGARET S. MAHLER SERIES

This series of yearly volumes began appearing in 1991 and is based upon the panel discussions presented at the prestigious Annual Margaret Mahler Symposia held in Philadelphia. Each volume consists of three papers and their discussions presented at the most recent Symposium. A thorough introduction and a comprehensive conclusion that pulls all the material together are specially written for the book. Occasionally, one or two papers that were not presented at the meeting but represent the cutting-edge thinking on the topic are also included. While this format and organization gives these books a friendly familiarity, the books' contents vary greatly and are invariably a source of excitement and clinical enthusiasm. Volumes published so far have addressed topics as diverse as hatred and cultural differences in childhood development, extramarital affairs and sibling relationship, mourning and self psychology, and resilience, and boundary violations. Among the distinguished psychoanalysts whose work has appeared in this series are Salman Akhtar, Anni Bergman, Harold Blum, Ruth Fischer, Alvin Frank, Dorothy Holmes, Otto Kernberg, Selma Kramer, Peter Neubauer, Henri Parens, Fred Pine, John Munder Ross, and Ernest Wolf, to name a few. The vantage point is always broad based and includes developmental, clinical, and cultural variables but the end point is consistently an enhancement of the technical armamentarium of the therapist.

BOOKS BASED UPON THE MARGARET S. MAHLER SYMPOSIA
Thicker Than Blood: Bonds of Fantasy and Reality in Adoption (1999)
  by Salman Akhtar and Selma Kramer
Does God Help? Developmental and Clinical Aspects of Religious Belief (2000) edited
  by Salman Akhtar and Henri Parens
Three Faces of Mourning: Melancholia, Manic Defense, and Moving On (2001) edited
  by Salman Akhtar
Real and Imaginary Fathers: Development, Transference, and Healing (2004) edited by
  Salman Akhtar and Henri Parens
The Language of Emotions: Developmental, Psychopathology, and Technique (2005)
  edited by Salman Akhtar and Harold P. Blum
Interpersonal Boundaries: Variations and Violations (2006) edited by Salman Akhtar
Listening to Others: Developmental and Clinical Aspects of Empathy and Attunement
  (2007) edited by Salman Akhtar
The Unbroken Soul: Tragedy, Trauma, and Human Resilience (2008) edited by Henri
  Parens, Harold P. Blum, Salman Akhtar
Lying, Cheating, and Carrying On: Developmental, Clinical, and Sociocultural Aspects
  of Dishonesty and Deceit (2009) by Salman Akhtar and Henri Parens
The Electrified Mind: Development, Psychopathology, and Treatment in the Era of Cell
  Phones and the Internet (2011) edited by Salman Akhtar
The Mother and Her Child: Clinical Aspects of Attachment, Separation, and Loss (2012)
  edited by Salman Akhtar
Guilt: Origins, Manifestations, and Management (2013) edited by Salman Akhtar
Human Goodness: Origins, Manifestations, and Management (2014) edited by
  Salman Akhtar
The New Motherhoods: Patterns of Early Child Care in Contemporary Culture (2015)
  edited by Salman Akhtar
Divorce: Emotional Impact and Therapeutic Interventions (2016) edited by
  Salman Akhtar

Divorce

Emotional Impact and Therapeutic Interventions

Edited by
Salman Akhtar

ROWMAN & LITTLEFIELD
Lanham • Boulder • New York • London

Published by Rowman & Littlefield
A wholly owned subsidiary of The Rowman & Littlefield Publishing Group, Inc.
4501 Forbes Boulevard, Suite 200, Lanham, Maryland 20706
www.rowman.com

Unit A, Whitacre Mews, 26-34 Stannary Street, London SE11 4AB

British Library Cataloguing in Publication Information Available

Library of Congress Cataloging-in-Publication Data
ISBN: 9781442279315 (cloth : alk. paper)
ISBN: 9781442279322 (pbk. : alk. paper)
ISBN: 9781442279339 (electronic)

♾™ The paper used in this publication meets the minimum requirements of American National Standard for Information Sciences—Permanence of Paper for Printed Library Materials, ANSI/NISO Z39.48-1992.

Printed in the United States of America

To the memory of Margaret S. Mahler and Selma Kramer

Contents

Acknowledgments

All the chapters in this book, except Chapters One and Eight, were originally presented as papers at the 47th Annual Margaret S. Mahler Symposium on Child Development, held on April 16, 2016. We wish to express gratitude to the Department of Psychiatry of Jefferson Medical College, the main sponsor of this event. We are especially indebted to Dr. Michael Vergare, Chairman of the Department of Psychiatry and Human Behavior of the Jefferson Medical College; Mary Etezady, Chair of the Board of the Psychoanalytic Foundation of the Psychoanalytic Center of Philadelphia; and William Singletary, President of the Margaret S. Mahler Foundation, for their continued kind support. There are many others who helped in subtle and not-so-subtle ways. To them, our most sincere thanks indeed. Finally, we wish to acknowledge deep appreciation of Ms. Jan Wright, for her superb organization of the symposium and for her skillful preparation of this book's manuscript.

Chapter One

The Emotional Impact of Divorce

An Overview

Salman Akhtar and Shawn Blue

Freud (1930) proposed that man is bound to remain somewhat unhappy since the forces of nature shall never come under his total control, his body will sooner or later betray him, and his relationships will fail to meet his expectations. The last mentioned source of man's "common unhappiness" (Freud, 1895, p. 305) is of central concern to the topic at hand, that is, the breakdown of the martial bond leading to divorce. Now, we know fully well that most religions and most societies allow for the dissolution of marriage if the relationship between the partners has turned sour and become insufferable. However, such religious and legal sanctions do little to preclude or dampen the pain and psychic disorganization that often accompanies divorce. It is also true that divorce is often the midpoint of an evolving story and not its beginning or its end.

Psychoanalysis, being relatively averse to hybrid concepts that cross over from the intrapsychic realm to the "interpsychic" (Bolognini, 2011), or "interpersonal" (Sullivan, 1953) spheres of life, has had little to say about marriage and divorce. The word "divorce" does not appear in the index to the *Standard Edition* of Freud's complete works but is mentioned twenty-nine times in the *Concordance* to his works (Guttman et al., 1980). Most of these entries are colloquial (e.g., "he got divorced") or figurative (e.g., "the divorce between sexual and ego instincts") and therefore of little technical value. However, a few entries do carry some weight. These include Freud's mention that a longing to get divorced can mobilize death wishes toward little children who are seen a barriers to such a decision (1901), that the early loss of a parent via divorce can result in over-involvement with the remaining parent and can "determine the sex of the person who is later chosen to be a sexual object" (1905, p. 230), and that divorce can precipitate anxiety symptoms (1910). Also noticeable is Freud's (1916–1917) well-known, if dated, statement that "we require him

1

[i.e. the patient] to postpone for the term of his treatment any vital decisions on choice of a profession, business undertakings, marriage or divorce, and only to put them in practice when the treatment is finished" (p. 434). While interesting, these passing observations do not actually tell much about the psychological antecedents and consequences of divorce. To learn about them, one has to turn to the more contemporary psychoanalysts, especially those who have devoted significant parts of their attention to adult psychological development (e.g., Erikson, 1950, 1982; Cath, 1965; Vaillant, 1977; Levinson et al., 1978; Colarusso and Nemiroff, 1981; Ross, 1994). It is from these sources and four psychoanalytically oriented monographs on divorce (Wallerstein and Blakeslee, 1989; Wallerstein, Lewis, and Blakeslee, 2000; Ehrlich, 2014; Leonoff, 2015) that the following portrait of the emotional impact of divorce is drawn. At times, material from additional sources has also been incorporated. Before proceeding with this agenda, however, we wish to provide some basic factual details about the incidence and prevalence of divorce.

EPIDEMIOLOGY

As everyone knows well, divorce is frequent in the United States and its occurrence is becoming more and more common. Nonetheless, one needs familiarity with the actual data in this realm to grasp the gravity of the problem. The following figures are taken from the United States Census Bureau Reports (2011, 2015).

- The overall national rates for every 1000 men over the past 12 months were 19.1 marriages, 9.2 divorces, and 3.5 instances of widowhood.
- The overall national rates for every 1000 women over the past 12 months were 17.6 marriages, 9.7 divorces, and 7.8 instances of widowhood.
- Women live longer and tend to marry older men. Therefore, widowhood rates are higher for women.
- The proportion of adults who marry only once has steadily declined (from 54 to 50% for men and from 60 to 54% for women).
- Men remarry more often than women.
- Non-Hispanic white men and women are most likely to have married three or more times while Asian men and women were least likely.
- Higher than average divorce rates for both men and women are mostly found in Southern states like Kentucky, Tennessee, Georgia, Alabama, Mississippi, Louisiana, Arkansas, and Texas. Lower than average rates are mostly found in Northeastern states like New Jersey, New York, Connecticut, Pennsylvania, and Massachusetts.
- A total of 1,100,401 children lived in the home of a parent who had divorced in the preceding twelve months.

- Children who lived with a parent divorced within the last year were more likely to be in a household with annual income below poverty level as compared with other children. The fact that most such children lived with their mothers partly explains the prevalence of poverty in such households; women have lower earning potential in the labor force.

This set of data impresses upon us that the problem of marital breakdown is a huge one. It affects a large number of adults and children and has multifaceted psychosocial implications. In simple words, divorce needs to be taken with utter seriousness.

ANTECEDENTS

In the hurry to consider the affective aftermath of divorce, one is tempted to overlook the cynicism and emotional deadness that precede the final break-up of a marriage. To be sure, there are incidences where divorce is precipitated by abrupt betrayal, discovery of "secret lives," and grotesque acts of violence. More often, divorce is the culmination of a slowly unfolding process of disillusionment, resentment, grudge holding, and undeniable estrangement between the partners. In other words, an "emotional divorce" precedes the actual or legal divorce. The atmosphere of the couple's home no longer bears any resemblance to its past harmony. Even the world outside begins to appear different. The following poem, titled *Events*, portrays the malevolent transformation well:

> Magicians put their hats on,
> left with their parrots, balls, rings, and rabbits.
> Merciless rays of sinking sun slit the throat of the Western sky.
> The world forgot Nazim Hikmat.
> Some people complained that sugar is no longer sweet.
> Bob and Rachel began treating each other
> with the kindness reserved for a neighbor's dog.

(Akhtar, 2014, p. 59)

The sorrow accompanying such loveless civility is even more eloquently captured by the renowned British novelist, Ian McEwan (1997), in the following passage:

We continued our daily round because little else seemed clear. We knew we had lost heart, we had lost our heart. We were loveless, or we had lost the trick of love, and we didn't know how to begin talking about it. We slept in the same bed, but we didn't embrace. We used the same bathroom, but we never saw each other naked. We were scrupulously casual because we knew that anything less—cold politeness, for example—would have exposed the charade and led us into the conflict we longed to avoid. What had once seemed natural, like lovemaking or long talks or silent companionship, now appeared as robustly contrived as Harrison's fourth sea clock, impossible as well as anachronistic to recreate. When I looked at her, brushing her hair or bending to retrieve a book from the floor, I remembered her beauty like some schoolbook fact got by heart. True, but not immediately relevant. And I could reconstruct myself in her own gaze as oafishly large and coarse, a biologically motivated bludgeon, a giant polyp of uninspired logic with which she was mistakenly associated. When I spoke to her, my voice rang dull and flat in my skull, and not just every sentence but every word was a lie. (p. 150)

Sooner or later, the "lie" falls apart and the two partners realize that their marriage has died. These literary portrayals of "emotional divorce" preceding the "actual divorce" have their operational counterparts in psychological literature. Kaslow (1991), for instance, has conceptualized a seven-stage model of divorce. The first stage is called the *emotional disengagement stage* and includes the period when the couple identifies conflict within the marital union. It is the point at which the couple acknowledges that the relationship is deteriorating. Kaslow suggests that disengagement occurs when there is a change in one of the partners—one of the partners changes too much in relation to the other partner—or the couple experiences trauma in the relationship that is unresolved. Couples typically seek psychotherapy at this stage as they experience anxiety and indecision. Couples who engage in couples' psychotherapy are more successful at resolving their conflict when each partner is also participating in individual psychotherapy (Whitaker and Miller, 1969; Kaslow, 1991). Also at this stage, psychotherapists can assist the couple in considering the effect of divorce on their children. However, once the decision to divorce has been made, both partners can utilize individual therapy to address feelings of loss and grief.

The second stage of the model is called the *legal divorce* and involves the actual legal components of the divorce. It also includes the financial and custodial agreements associated with divorce. As an alternative to a litigated civil divorce, the couple can consider mediation. Family systems theory is in line with the mediation process because it takes into consideration the well-being of all those involved. Mediation allows the couple to collaborate and make decisions that are best for their family as opposed to the litigated civil process, which is facilitated by attorneys and a judge and ultimately can lead to feelings of helplessness and pessimism. In addition, with the litigated process, the couple can experience grief related to the loss of the family unit as well as financial and material possessions (Kaslow, 1991).

The third stage of this model includes the *economic divorce* and the couple begins to evaluate and manage financial matters. The fourth stage is called the *coparental divorce* and includes issues related to custody of the children. The value of this stage allows the couple to consider the true impact of the divorce on the children and to acknowledge the loss experienced by children. Divorced parents are reminded to have children's needs remain the focus. The coparenting plan should continuously be evaluated to see if modifications need to be made (Kaslow, 1991).

The fifth stage is called the *community divorce*. It includes the period where the family begins to redefine old social networks and seek out new social supports. In addition, the family creates a new routine and lifestyle. The sixth stage is called the *religious divorce*. The divorced couple can consider a divorce ceremony in order to have a religious divorce, in addition to the legal one. The final stage is the *psychic divorce*. The family continues to enjoy new activities and interests. Divorced couples can consider new romantic partners. During this stage, the divorced individuals begin to rethink and revise their various roles. The divorced individuals seek understanding to their internal conflict and loss experienced from the divorce. In addition, they encourage the children to also grieve the loss of the divorce and avoid utilizing children as surrogate attachment figures for emotional and logistical support (Kaslow, 1991).

Wallerstein and Blakeslee (2003) offer another model of divorce and describe three stages. The first stage of *decision* occurs once the couple has elected to the start the process of divorce and can last anywhere from several months to a couple of years. It involves feelings of anger, sexual desire, and depression. The family unit becomes disrupted. The second stage of *transition* involves the development of a new family framework. Family members attempt to create new routines and a new lifestyle. Many revisions are made as the new family continues to solidify its new structure. Boundaries are tested and transitions are experienced during this stage. The third stage of *reconstitution* includes the new family as a stable and secure unit (Wallerstein and Blakeslee, 2003).

EMOTIONAL CONSEQUENCES

We will now focus upon the destabilizing impact of divorce on the marital partners, their children, other family members, friends, neighbors, and community-at-large as well. We will take up these radiating effects separately in the following passages, knowing fully well that the impact upon spouses, children, and other relatives and friends does not exist in isolation; in fact, there is much criss-cross and dialectical feedback involved here. Our separation of the emotional trauma of divorce into such categories is largely in the service of didactic clarity.

Spouses

The most important task involved in the aftermath of divorce involves mourning. This mourning involves not only loss of the relationship but also loss of the bond, which includes the shared routine and life of the divorced couple (Ehrlich, 2014). As with all romantic relationship dissolutions, but especially in the case of divorce, this can include all real and symbolic shared experiences. In addition to mourning, obtaining a new sense of identity or redefining oneself signals healthy functioning after divorce. Mourning also involves divorced adults revising roles and addressing traumatic reactions to the divorce (Wallerstein and Blakeslee, 2003). Psychological internal distress will most likely continue when one does not adequately mourn his or her divorce. Negative consequences of not mourning include denial, preoccupation with the former spouse and conflict (Wallerstein and Blakeslee, 2003).

Attachment plays a major role in the experience of loss during a divorce (Feeney and Monin, 2008; Ehrlich, 2014). Feeney and Monin (2008) describe divorce as "the disruption of one of the strongest affectional bonds formed by parents" (Feeney and Monin, 2008, p. 934). Using an attachment perspective to conceptualize divorce, these authors argue that marriage involves an available and trustworthy partner who provides safety, comfort, and support as well as encouragement to explore one's world. In addition, marriage includes both individuals being able to identify the trustworthiness of the other partner and to build a healthy, rewarding, and functioning relationship together. According to this theory, divorce would occur when these qualities are no longer present in the relationship.

The loss experienced as a result of divorce causes the divorced couple to have feelings of anxiety, anger, depression, and detachment (Bowlby, 1973, 1979; Feeney and Monin, 2008). Furthermore, divorce results in higher incidences of physical problems and mental health distress when compared to happily married couples (Blumenthal, 1967; Gove, 1973; Verbrugge, 1979; Mirowsky and Ross, 2003; Feeney and Monin, 2008). Physical problems and mental health distress affects both divorced men and women. However, it appears that men and women experience different areas of distress. Women tend to experience distress related to economic challenges (Lillard and Waite, 1995) as well as distress experienced in the marriage (Gottman, 1994). Men tend to experience physical and mental health complications due to the loss of social support (Umberson, 1987; Gove and Shin, 1989) and feelings of loneliness (Gottman, 1994). However, despite the emotional and physical manifestations that occur after a divorce, many adults are able to effectively manage the consequences of divorce (Booth and Amato, 1991; Aseltine and Kessley, 1993; Amato, 2000; Hetherington and Kelly, 2002; Sbarra and Emery, 2005; Feeney and Monin, 2008).

Bowlby (1979) contends that adults react to separation and loss and experience feelings of numbness, yearning and seeking, disorganization, and despair and reorganization. Adjustment is further disrupted when the previous marriage included ambivalence. In addition, if the previous marriage involved a partner who encouraged positive self-esteem properties or if another attachment figure besides the ex-spouse is lacking, the functioning of divorced individuals is impacted. As a result, it is conceptualized that those divorced individuals with a secure attachment style will fare better due to their internal working models and because they tend to have more effective coping strategies and social support systems, when compared to divorced individuals with insecure attachment styles (Bowlby, 1979; Feeney and Monin, 2008). Divorce tends to be more difficult for individuals who have an insecure attachment style history (Bowlby, 1979). This is due to a reinforcement of the insecure attachment style's working models of relationships and due to activation of earlier separations and losses.

The decision to divorce rarely occurs mutually as a simultaneous act. Even if both spouses eventually come to a mutual decision, there is often one spouse who initiates conflict and the proposition to separate. As a result, divorced individuals experience differing adjustment dependent upon who initiated the divorce. Better adjustment tends to be associated with those individuals who initiate the divorce (Gray and Silver, 1990; Kitson, 1982).

It appears that continued contact with a divorced spouse causes additional stress (Bohannon, 1970; Weiss, 1975, 1976; Hetherington, Cox, and Cox, 1982; Kitson and Morgan, 1990; Duran-Aydintug, 1998). Divorced individuals experience many conflicting feelings that often cause confusion and leads to a desire for continued contact with the divorced ex-spouse (Weiss, 1975; Berman, 1988a, 1988b). In addition, divorced individuals continue to feel attachment toward their ex-spouse (Goode, 1956; Weiss, 1975; Spanier and Castro, 1979; Brown, Felton, Whiteman, and Manela, 1980; Kitson, 1982; Berman, 1988b). It is theorized that these feelings of attachment lead to the physical and emotional disruption that is experienced during and after a divorce (Weiss, 1976; Brown et al., 1980; Kitson, 1982; Berman, 1988a, 1988b). When a divorce occurs, divorced individuals experience separation anxiety and this leads to activation of the attachment system (Bowlby, 1973, 1979). Once the attachment system is activated, divorced individuals will employ interventions to seek proximity to their attachment figure (Bowlby, 1982), which remains their ex-spouse. In adapting to the loss, divorced individuals are challenged by the conflicting goals of seeking proximity to the lost attachment figure (i.e., ex-spouse) and detaching from the ex-spouse (Mikulincer and Florian, 1996).

Other research shows positive aspects of continued attachment with ex-spouses (Masheter, 1990, 1991). Most importantly, a cooperative parenting arrangement among ex-spouses can reduce feelings of loss (Hetherington and Camara, 1984; Masheter, 1991). The key to improving the chances of positive results in the event of frequent contact after divorce is to engage in constructive behaviors, especially in situations of co-parenting (Emery, 1988; Furstenberg and Cherlin, 1991; Masheter, 1991; Madden-Derdich and Ardetti, 1999; Feeney and Monin, 2008). Furthermore, Reibstein (1998) suggests that continued contact among ex-spouses should be limited and rule-bound. In order to establish boundaries in the relationship and increase the probability that the contact will have positive results, it is suggested that ex-spouses redefine their relationships. One way this can occur is by revising the attachment bond to an affiliative bond (Cassidy, 2008). Ex-spouses would maintain their parenting duties but would not engage in the activities of the previous attachment behavior (i.e., utilizing the ex-spouse as an attachment figure or a sexual partner).

Wallerstein and Blakeslee (2003) contend that there are two psychological tasks that adults must address during divorce: to re-create a new life and to care for and parent the children. Divorced couples not only experience loss of the significant other, they also experience loss of any children, as the family unit is modified (Ehrlich, 2014). Family members experience loss from the divorce but also continue to experience it with the repetition (or sometimes permanent) loss experienced by custodial agreements (Ehrlich, 2014). There are several interventions that divorced parents can employ to improve the well-being and functioning of children after divorce. Ehrlich (2014) describes how post-divorce planning, communication with children, and post-divorce co-parenting are all beneficial in helping children adapt to divorce. Ehrlich (2014) further suggests a post-divorce parenting arrangement plan that is created before communicating to children about the upcoming divorce. A mental health professional with divorce expertise can be consulted when parents experience conflict that they are unable to resolve. In addition, parents commit to not further contributing to the conflict that children experience by not having disputes in the presence of children and communicating in a respectful manner when discussing the other parent. Next, parents communicate with children about the divorce as well as the post-divorce parenting plan. Children are encouraged to express their grief related to the divorce but are also provided with encouragement and reassurance. Finally, parents check in after the divorce occurs to monitor how children are managing the emotional and logistical consequences of the divorce. If needed, the parents consult with a mental health professional about how to best help a child manage his or her experience. Additionally, parents are aware of their own emotional experiences and seek treatment, if needed (Ehrlich, 2014).

In situations of children acting out as a result of divorce, parents mistakenly focus on the dysfunctional behavior instead of addressing the grief underlying the behavior (Ehrlich, 2014). Parents must be prepared to accept the child's experience even if it contains difficult feelings such as disappointment, anger, and betrayal. Parents must also be able to manage their own grief regarding the divorce while also being able to manage their child's, as well as assist the child in building affect regulation skills. A parent's ability to effectively manage their emotional experience to divorce has an important role in their ability to be empathic to their children (Ehrlich, 2014). Parents who exercised skill before the divorce are often able to exhibit empathy post-divorce. However, those parents who have a deficit in the skill of empathy often have great difficulty exhibiting this skill post-divorce.

During mourning of a divorce, divorced parents experience emotional conflict related to the divorced spouse (Ehrlich, 2014). Immediately after the divorce, divorced parents often experience painful feelings when remembering the positive qualities of their former spouse. Furthermore, divorced parents also experience difficulty sharing in their children's excitement related to positive events that occur in the other divorced parent's home. This can make it difficult for divorced parents to be emotionally available to their children who often need extra support following the divorce. Instead of avoiding these conversations, it is recommended that divorced parents discuss feelings of anger and disappointment, especially in situations of abandonment or violence (Tessman, 1996). However, parents are cautioned to not endorse their own conclusions related to the divorce but to provide a realistic evaluation of the child's experience of the divorce (Ehrlich, 2014). Divorced parents are often ill equipped at being able to effectively manage their child's complaints regarding their interactions with their parents (Ehrlich, 2014). Divorced parents who have effectively mourned their divorce will be better able to handle conversations with their children and not introduce their own emotional agendas.

It has been argued that parenting arrangements are fairer to divorced parents than to the children (Ehrlich, 2014). Often the children's emotional needs are not the priority when negotiating parental custodial arrangements. Conflict occurs when divorced parents are unable to manage the loss associated with the divorce. Divorced parents who experience interpersonal conflict often do so as a result of a desire to address an injustice. These individuals also engage in projection as a defense mechanism which, when not appropriately communicated, can lead to conflict. Another defensive behavior that can lead to conflict in divorced couples is splitting. In addition, the use of defensive behaviors by divorced couples leads to lowered empathy, moral functioning, and self-reflection (Ehrlich, 2014).

How a divorced family reacts after a divorce is mostly predicted by the way the divorced couple handles the actual process of divorce, as well as how conflict was managed during the marriage (Wallerstein and Blakeslee, 2003).

Therefore, it is important for the divorced couple to go through the process of divorce with integrity and compassion. This process involves putting aside self-interest and evaluating and addressing the needs of the children.

Leonoff (2015) contends that during a marriage, the couple creates a symbolic baby. This baby incorporates a shared vision of the romantic union and is necessary in order for the relationship to thrive. The couple births a real child (either biologically or through adoption) and the creative energy between the couple forms the foundation for the identity of the child. All that is required is a couple that mutually creates the intention to birth a child.

When a couple comes to the decision to divorce, grief and loss are experienced as this creative energy is extinguished. The relationship can no longer survive because the shared vision has been broken. The couple no longer derives energy from the symbolic baby and or the actual child(ren) to maintain the relationship. The children and the family are forced to revise their identity as the original one has been challenged. Leonoff (2015) insists that divorce provides an opportunity for reflection. Reflection allows one to gain meaning and insight and provides an opportunity for accountability, as well as a return to individuality. Reflection allows divorced individuals to grieve their losses, to revise their identities, to address their intrapersonal and interpersonal dynamics, and to care for their children.

Divorced individuals have to attend to multiple tasks when experiencing divorce. First, individuals must address their personal conflict related to the divorce. They must manage symptoms of grief and loss of what occurred in the marriage but also in the process of the divorce. Loss related to the disruption of their main attachment figure must be acknowledged and addressed, as well as the disruption to relationships with any children. Attachment trauma related to the divorced individuals' working models of relationships must also be worked through (abandonment, trustworthiness, etc.). Individuals must also address grief related to the vision of a shared life that now requires revision.

Kaslow (1991) suggests that divorced individuals need to consider their own ego functioning and use of defenses during the process of a divorce. In addition, developmental maturity and conflict related to one's childhood and family of origin must be evaluated and resolved. If these areas are not adequately addressed, they can lead to poorer adjustment during divorce but can also manifest itself in the type of behaviors and communication exhibited during the divorce. Another task necessary of this time of personal reflection involves one's identity related to one's religious beliefs. Divorced individuals must deal with their personal conflict related to their divorce and religious views, but must also attend to any conflict experienced by their religious institution, religious leader, and the other members of the religious community. Kaslow (1991) suggests that divorced individuals can consider having a divorce ceremony that incorporates the religious and spiritual aspects of the union as well as provide an opportunity for the family to honor the relationship.

In addition to all of the aforementioned personal issues that need to be attended to, divorced individuals must also be aware of and address the emotional, physical, and logistical issues of the child(ren). Separating one's personal issues from the child's needs can only be completed with successful introspection and insight into the divorced individual's experience. Only then will divorced individuals have the emotional capacity and availability to maintain the child(ren)'s needs as the main priority. Collaboration with the ex-spouse in a manner that is respectful and sensitive will improve the adjustment of children post-divorce. In addition, serious consideration and planning of the parenting plan, with needed revisions when needed are crucial to the development of the child(ren).

Children

It is argued that children might experience more devastating effects from divorce than their parents (Feeney and Monin, 2008). This is supported by the fact that children lack control over the parents' decision to become divorced and the divorce often occurs unexpectedly. Children experience loss related to their parents and original family structure, but also with friends, extended family members, and other numerous attachment figures (Johnson, 1988).

Divorce exerts problematic effects on both psychological and physical health for children. However, a closer look shows that certain factors play a part in explaining the effect on children's psychological and physical health. More than divorce itself, the quality of the parental marriage and family interactions has more of an impact on children's functioning. However, how parents react during the divorce often mimics behaviors and interactions experienced during the marriage. In addition, maternal depression and a fear of being abandoned have important implications on how children adapt after divorce. Finally, the lack of a social support system has negative effects on children's development.

Children often have a myriad of consequences that can negatively impact their functioning after a divorce (Wallerstein and Blakeslee, 2003). It is argued that children of divorce must achieve developmental tasks that do not exist in non-divorced families. Children can experience additional logistical and emotional responsibilities such as taking care of siblings and/or a divorced parent who is grieving or managing poorly after the divorce. Consequences can also occur to children's academic and social lives. To avoid becoming parentified, divorced parents must make attempts to allow children to have experiences relevant to their developmental level.

Children become further parentified when divorced parents modify their relationships with their children (Ehrlich, 2014). The nature of the relationship changes (Johnston and Campbell, 1988) and challenges children to provide emotional support to divorced parents and to execute tasks left uncompleted by the divorced parent (Hodges, 1991; Ehrlich, 2014). This can disrupt children's developmental maturity and thwart appropriate separation (Kalter, 1990; Ehrlich, 2014), autonomy (Wallerstein and Blakeslee, 1989; Ehrlich, 2014) and healthy interpersonal relationships (Ehrlich, 2014).

Divorce has an effect on a child's attachment security (Bowlby, 1973, 1980, 1982; Feeney and Monin, 2008). More specifically, children lose security in their parents' comfort, trustworthiness, support, availability, and protection. As a result, children tend to integrate the conflict experienced in the parental marriage and divorce into their identity, their working models of relationships, and within their internal models of interpersonal dynamics. One important consequence of divorce on development focuses on the attachment style of children (Feeney and Monin, 2008). Young adult children of divorce seem to fare best when either the mother or both parents remarry. In addition, attachment security was higher for young adult children of divorce if they believed that they were not the reason for their parent's divorce. Finally, the quality of the divorced parents' relationships with children of divorce plays a major role in their functioning. Divorced fathers' attachment with their children, especially in the case of male children, often results in sons experiencing more psychological distress when compared to daughters (Hetherington, Cox, and Cox, 1978). Daughters, on the other hand, have a tendency to exhibit caretaking behaviors with their fathers (Hetherington et al., 1978; Bretherton, Ridgeway and Cassidy, 1990; Page and Bretherton, 2001, 2003; Bretherton and Page, 2004).

Children often experience feelings of self-blame, guilt, and shame in the event of parental divorce (Ehrlich, 2014). In addition, children can develop a feeling of helplessness (Ehrlich, 2014) as a result of the inability to solve parental conflicts and disputes. Furthermore, children of parental divorce often experience a sense of loneliness (Marquardt, 2005; Ehrlich, 2014). This occurs as a result of their loss not being validated by parents and others. In addition, children often become parentified, which can lead to a feeling of aloneness. The tendency for children from divorced families to experience self-blame is unfortunate, especially because this emotional outcome is associated with poor adjustment (Healy, Stewart, and Copeland, 1993; Bussell, 1995).

The developmental period and age of children is important in understanding a child's reaction to divorce. In addition, the child's age will also determine the type of behaviors they will engage in as well as their level of coping skills, reasoning ability, and fears related to security and stability (Wallerstein and Blakeslee, 2003). Children haven't yet developed the skills to rationally understand the process of divorce as well as be well equipped to effectively regulate their affect. As a way to manage this conflict, children often employ defensive behaviors such as displacement, somatization, detachment, withdrawal, and intellectualization. The outcome of these defensive behaviors serves a role in the avoidance of feelings of sadness, anxiety, and helplessness. Children also engage in denial, another defensive behavior, by identifying with the absent parent. This behavior serves the role of counteracting the feeling of loss (Kalter, 1990; Tessman, 1996; Ehrlich, 2014).

Defensive behaviors have both emotional adaptive outcomes as well as negative outcomes related to functioning (Ehrlich, 2014). Children are challenged through the use of defensive behaviors to seek insight into intrapersonal conflicts and in some situations can serve as a protective mechanism for discordant feelings. However, the use of defensive posturing can also lead to poor affect regulation. It also might cause children to fail to utilize self-soothing skills or to initiate aid when needed. Children's inability to regulate affect not only effects their development in childhood but can persist in adulthood with an added deficit in interpersonal relating (Ehrlich, 2014). Children of divorce experience better adjustment when they utilize constructive behaviors including the use of problem-solving skills and initiating social support networks when compared to children of divorce who engage in avoidance behaviors (Sandler, Tein, and West, 1994).

Parental divorce has a significant influence on how children psychologically make sense of themselves and the world. For example, witnessing parental marital failure often leads children to believe that they will have future failures themselves (Wallerstein and Blakeslee, 2003). In addition, if infidelity occurred in the marital relationship, children can view parents and others as untrustworthy. Furthermore, when children begin to create their moral identity, they experience an internal struggle with how to resolve conflict as a result of parental immorality (Wallerstein, Lewis, and Blakeslee, 2000). Children who are able to create their own morality system despite any conflict experienced in the parental marriage and divorce will be able to navigate future dilemmas related to moral values.

One important aspect related to the functioning of children after a divorce involves the way in which the divorce is communicated by parents (Ehrlich, 2014). Often divorce is unexpected and children are surprised by the news of their parents' conflict. In addition, children are often told in an unpremeditated manner and are often provided communication that lacks details or reassurance (Ehrlich, 2014). Without an adequate understanding of the divorce, children can create fantasies as they fear events that could occur to themselves or their parents (Wallerstein and Blakeslee, 2003). Having a realistic understanding of the consequences of divorce and the parent's plan for how to structure their world post-divorce allows children to adapt follow-ing the divorce. In addition, when divorce is not discussed in a meaningful way between divorced parents and children, emotional detachment remains within the relationship. Its presence is felt and not discussed, and the ambi-guity causes emotional distance in the parent/child relationship (Wallerstein, Lewis, and Blakeslee, 2000).

Whereas children used to navigate one household with one unified value and rule system, when divorce occurs, children must now begin to negotiate two households with sometimes varying rules and values (Ehrlich, 2014). This variation can cause conflict for children as they attempt to make sense of and operate in both environments (Marquardt, 2005; Finley and Schwartz, 2010; Ehrlich, 2014). Additionally, children often face a question of loyalty when divorce occurs as they negotiate their interactions with both parents (Ehrlich, 2014). Given the symbolic and actual safety and comfort that a child's familiar home can bring, the need to transition to an unfamiliar new lodging with one of their parents can cause conflict (Ehrlich, 2014). It is help-ful for children to return to their normal routines and activities following a divorce (Wallerstein and Blakeslee, 2003). Doing so can provide stability in the midst of the disruption caused by parental divorce.

The relationship of parents on children's adjustment remains important even after the divorce (Ahrons, 2007). Children who experience conflict between their divorced parents often have feelings of being overwhelmed and helpless (Ehrlich, 2014). Engaging in cooperative parenting behaviors among divorced parents is linked to better relationships with parents into adulthood, as well as with extended family members (i.e., grandparents, stepparents, siblings). Children report an understanding that their divorced parents might not end up as friends; however, they desire that their parents refrain from causing conflict and discussing each other in a derogatory way. Children, even as adults, wish for their parents to interact in a healthy manner. When special events occur, adult children are challenged to make decisions about how to involve divorced parents in their lives, in an attempt to share these events with both parents. Many events that should be focused on the children (i.e., birthdays, weddings, etc.) often are misaligned as adult children try to manage parental conflict. Often, adult children choose to involve both parents or to leave one or both parents out (Ahrons, 2007).

After divorce, if one or both of divorced parents remarry, children are tasked with the responsibility of adopting a new family structure. This new structure involves navigating new relationships with stepparents, stepsib-lings, and half-siblings. When children are already trying to manage their emotional experience and adjustment related to the divorce, the added impact of introducing new loyalties to new family members can cause distress. New parental romantic partners can cause children to feel as if they have to negotiate what already feels like limited time with the divorced parent. In addition, new partners often squash children's hope that their parents might one day reunite. Finally, becoming close to new parental partners can cause children to experience a conflict of loyalty. Alternatively, children might avoid becoming close with the parent again with the fear that they will be judged as being disloyal (Ehrlich, 2014).

The original (biological or adopted) family serves as a framework for the child's identity. The original family reflects the child's structure of the love shared by the parents and for the child. Encouraging children to quickly adopt new family structures can be perceived as denial of the original family, and denial of the child's identity. When the original family is replaced by a new family, this causes conflict and grief for the child. When divorce occurs, it is important for parents to respect and validate the original family for the child in order to sustain the child's identity. Leonoff (2015) suggests that divorce and remarriages could potentially help children operate in a pluralistic world. Furthermore, it creates an opportunity for a new definition of family and how new relationships can merge to create a familial bond. However, it is important for divorced parents to support and nurture the original family as well as the new family.

When divorce occurs, parents must begin to conceptualize the new separated homes as one system (Leonoff, 2015). To leave them separated and unaffected by each other adds to the child's sense of loss and increases feelings of insecurity and instability. Seeing all homes as one system adds to children's sense of identity and definition and helps them navigate their new environments. It creates a cohesive environment and along with cooperative parenting, improves the adjustment of children. Not communicating in a sensitive and respectful manner toward or about the ex-spouse can have detrimental results related to children's emotional development. The impact of hearing derogatory comments makes the child feel as if they are in some way *bad* due to their shared genetic background and in some cases reinforces the child's notion that he or she is somehow to blame for the marital dissolution.

To further increase the child's sense of stability, the divorced parents must direct all care and focus to their children and their new experiences, relationships, and environments. Parents must consider the child's grief and loss related to the divorce in addition to helping ensure the child's relationships and environments are conducive to the child's needs. Parents can also allow children to help in decision making, which allows children to feel as if they have an important role in the family. Furthermore, it allows children to feel less helpless (Wallerstein and Blakeslee, 2003). With remarriages, it is also important to acknowledge the coinciding additional stress, conflict, and loss that they incur. The importance of this planning and relationship building is important before, during, and after the divorce. Additionally, it is important to maintain into the child's adulthood. Divorced parents success during childhood can have lasting effects on the adult parent/child relationship.

One evidence of such detrimental effect comes in the form of the "sleeper effect" (Wallerstein and Blakeslee, 1989, pp. 56–64). This refers to the resurgence of conflicts originally mobilized by the parental divorce at a time when children are entering adulthood and establishing their own romantic partnerships.

> The sleeper effect primarily affects young women, in part because girls seem to fare much better psychologically immediately after divorce than boys. Because girls appear so much better adjusted socially, academically, and emotionally every step of the way after divorce, much of the research about the effects of divorce on children emphasizes the good recovery of girls compared with the more troubled experience of boys.
>
> As young men enter adulthood, their behavior is more congruent with their pasts, reflecting difficulties encountered throughout their high school years. Many girls may seem relatively well adjusted even through high school and then—wham! Just as they undertake the passage to adulthood and their own first serious relationships, they encounter the sleeper effect. We have not seen a counterpart of the sleeper effect among boys, nor do boys have as much anxiety over relationships with girls. (Wallerstein and Blakeslee, 1989, p. 63)

Other authors (Barber, 1988; Evans and Bloom, 1996; Feeney and Monin, 2008) have also noticed a gender difference in how children of divorce are influenced later in life. According to them, male adult children of divorce tend to be more securely attached when compared to female adult children of divorce; this observation is in accordance with the Wallerstein and Blakeslee (1989) comment cited above.

All in all, it should be remembered that divorced parents have bequeathed a model of shattered marriage to their offspring. Thus, when children of divorce grow up and approach opportunities for love, they lack a model of secure love and intimacy and either never obtain it or create it through experiences of subsequent healthy relationships. As a result, children are left with certain psychological dilemmas to resolve related to fears and anxieties of betrayal, abandonment and trustworthiness, as well as conflicts of success and failure. Children must overcome these dilemmas in order to maintain a healthy model of love. Successfully mourning a past experience of parental divorce will enhance their future romantic relationships. This allows for a "second chance" for children in building healthy future romantic relationships (Wallerstein and Blakeslee, 2003).

Others

Divorce not only impacts the marital dyad but also affects other family members, friends, religious community, and even the society at large. All family members sooner or later have to readjust their relationships with the divorced couple. Grandparents, specifically, are typically a source of emotional support during conflict in the family (Barranti, 1985; Denham and Smith, 1989; Johnson and Barer, 1987). Many grandparents are unaware that a divorced couple has decided to start the process of a divorce (Cherlin and Furstenberg, 1986). As a result, the task for grandparents becomes adjusting both to their children's marital dissolution and to the affected relationship with their grandchildren. For those grandparents who had little contact or emotional investment in their grandchildren's lives, a divorce can maintain this distance and further separate the grandparent/grandchild relationship (Myers and Perrin, 1993). In some cases, due to animosity experienced between the divorced couple, grandparents might experience the loss of contact with grandchildren as the ex-couple attempts to punish each other.

Grandparents can experience conflict related to their identity and role as grandparent when divorce occurs (Myers and Perrin, 1993). Grandparents may experience grief, distress, and ambiguity (Denham and Smith, 1989; Sanders and Trygstad, 1989) related to the impacted relationships with both children and grandchildren. In addition, they will consider a loss related to their biological (or adopted) ties to their family. When remarriages occur, children's familial network increases and, as a result, grandparents have to negotiate time related to contact due to having to share grandchildren with their growing familial figures.

Grandparents can be sought out by divorced children to provide support during a divorce (Myers and Perrin, 1993). This support can be obtained emotionally, financially, and logistically. Grandparents have even taken on roles as surrogate parents in situations of divorce (Matthews and Sprey, 1984). In some cases, the added reliance on grandparents during a divorce can trigger childhood and familial conflicts between grandparent and adult child and can exacerbate an already stressful process. As grandparents offer additional support and take on additional roles, they can experience stress related to the financial and emotional strain. Furthermore, grandparents may be unable to participate in desired activities and other roles due to the added time investment to children and grandchildren (Myers and Perrin, 1993).

Friends of divorced couples find themselves in a situation where they must choose which spouse they wish to maintain their friendship. Some divorced couples will withdraw socially due to experiencing grief from the divorce, from fear of judgment by friends or concerns related to the potential of having mutual activities with the spouse. In addition, interactions with mutual friends and participating in activities once shared with divorced spouses can cause emotional discomfort (Morgan, Carder, and Neal, 1997).

Several factors play a role in whether divorced couples will gain support from social networks. It appears that the divorced individual who did not initiate the divorce tends to utilize others to gain emotional support (Duran-Aydintug, 1998; Thuen and Eikeland, 1998). In addition, the qualities of the divorced spouse also influences the amount of social support received. Being extroverted and emotionally stable (Lang, Staudinger, and Cartensen, 1998) as well as having a strong self-esteem (Smerglia, Miller, and Kort-Butler, 1999) all increase the chances that a divorced spouse will initiate support from others. In addition, having a higher level of education increases the size of one's networks (Campbell, Marsden, and Hurlbert, 1986; Moore, 1990). Furthermore, employment increases the chances of obtaining support from coworkers and colleagues (Baruch, Biener, and Barrett, 1987). In terms of gender, divorced women typically seek social support from family members and friends from their social group; divorced men usually seek out new relationships, especially a new romantic relationship (Gerstel, 1998; Rands, 1988).

As a result of divorce, divorced individuals experience transitions related to economic security and the home environment. Some individuals are forced to consider relocating in order to adjust to the new financial situation. This can influence the divorced individual's social network if he or she decides to move away from their previous home and lowers opportunities to engage with local friends. On the other hand, a new environment and neighborhood increase the opportunity to build new friendships (Larner, 1990; Magdol, 2000).

Divorce is a process that impacts society and the members of it. Based off of a historical framework of marriage and the family, divorce previously was viewed by society as being negative and carried stigma (Gibbs, 1969; Stack, 1980, 1990). As more individuals experience divorce, this stigmatization has lessened (Gibbs, 1969; Stack, 1980, 1990). Historical models that reflect the culture of its time period represent family units that include two parent biological families. However, with the existence of divorce and with a more accepting view of the structure of family, single-parent households, same-sex parent households, and blended families, these historical models have become modified.

Culture also influences the experience of divorce. Whether one adopts a collectivistic or individualistic approach will determine how the culture will view the divorce but will also determine the amount of support they provide (Triandis, Bontempo, Villareal, Asai, and Lucca, 1988). It is assumed that conflict can arise for individuals who are within a particular culture but hold different views than the culture. In the case of divorce, this can affect the emotional experience of divorced individuals but can also influence the amount of support provided.

Religion can play a major role in situations of divorce. A divorced individual could experience distress as they attempt to negotiate their religious views when experiencing a divorce. This can be exacerbated in cases when divorce is not accepted within the divorced individuals' religious community. Furthermore, if the religious community does not accept divorce, the religious leader and community members might resist providing support. Alternatively, the religious community could reinforce messages that lead to divorced individuals feeling judged for their circumstance.

Both family and friends of the divorced family are affected by the divorce as well, and their relationships can be modified in many different ways. Divorced individuals are tasked with the process of evaluating which friendships will endure the divorce (Leonoff, 2015). Other friendships that might not have been previously considered close could evolve into stronger relationships. The merging of relationships to build a stepfamily can be difficult and takes time for everyone to adjust and eventually to build the bond. Stepfamilies can increase their success when they spend considerable time and effort in building the relationships. Despite how difficult it can be to build the relationships within a stepfamily, there are also many benefits that occur socially, economically, and emotionally. One is reminded that when stepparents join the family, they do not automatically replace biological parents (Wallerstein, Lewis, and Blakeslee, 2000). Parents cannot be replaced, but their authentic relationships can be honored. Each individual relationship can be respected on its own merit.

THREE SPECIAL SITUATIONS

While the wide-ranging turmoil associated with divorce elucidated in the preceding sections of our contribution is applicable to more or less all those undergoing the crisis, three specific populations deserve extra attention. These involve the occurrence of divorce among same-sex couples, among immigrants (especially those who have freshly arrived in a new country), and among psychotherapists and psychoanalysts. The first group, for which pertinent data is just beginning to emerge, is already the target of social prejudice and thus carries an additional burden; break-up of close bonds, including that of marriage, can therefore be quite destabilizing. The second group is more vulnerable to the complications of divorce since it is already struggling with the mental pain and disorienting anxieties of geocultural dislocation. The third group is more vulnerable since it is exposed, on a daily basis, to serve as a "container" (Bion, 1963) of others' repudiated anxieties and unbearable affects. Facing divorce, the first two groups can experience psychic devasta-tion, while the third group can adversely affect those under its care and pro-tection. To be sure, the groups are not entirely separate and individuals can belong to more than one of them at the same time. Nonetheless, for didactic clarity, it is handy to discuss their problems independently.

Divorce among Same-Sex Couples

In 2015, a monumental decision was made by the Supreme Court to consti-tutionally allow same-gendered individuals to marry. This decision reflects a long battle to allow same-sex marriages, beginning in 1995 when Utah iden-tified itself as the first state to enforce a Defense of Marriage Act (DOMA) as well as 2003 when Massachusetts became the first state to make same-sex marriages legal. The power of this decision is highlighted by the legalization of same-sex couples to enjoy the same rights that have long been provided to heterosexual couples.

Study of the dissolution of same-sex couples is difficult for many reasons. Marriage for same-sex couples has only recently been granted for the entire nation. Therefore, most same-sex couples have not had the opportunity to marry and, as a result, to divorce. In addition, even among same-sex couples that have married, there is not much study of those who have entered into the divorce process. Moreover, there is not a great deal of research related to the dissolution of romantic relationships in same-sex individuals (Mohr, 2008). Much of the research available is based on bereavement related to the death of romantic partners as a result of acquired immune deficiency syndrome (AIDS). The available research is problematic due to most studies examin-ing romantic relationship dissolution of same-sex couples who are unmarried but yet are often compared to heterosexual married couples (or heterosexual unmarried couples who could legally marry if they chose to do so).

Same-sex couples and heterosexual couples have many similarities in their romantic unions, such as level of attachment, commitment, intimacy, and satisfaction (Kurdek, 2005; Herek, 2006; Mohr, 2008). Same-sex couples tend to differ from heterosexual couples regarding their division of household chores and these couples find more importance in equitable roles within the romantic relationship (Kurdek, 2005). In addition, same-sex couples receive less social support from family members (Kurdek, 2004; Herek, 2006). In light of less perceived support from family, same-sex couples tend to seek bolstering from friends in support of their relationships (Kurdek, 2004; Herek, 2006). Furthermore, same-sex couples appear to have more effective conflict-resolution skills when compared to heterosexual couples (Gottman et al., 2003; Kurdek, 2005). Same-sex male couples also express open com-munication regarding the exclusivity of their romantic unions (Peplau and

Spalding, 2000; Herek, 2006). On the other hand, same-sex male couples who had civil unions tended to not have sexual partners outside the relationship when compared to same-sex males who cohabitated (Solomon, Rothblum, and Balsam, 2005; Herek, 2006).

Same-sex couples appear to end their romantic relationships at a greater frequency than heterosexual couples, and that is potentially attributed to the historical lack of formal barriers, such as marriage and ultimately divorce (Kurdek, 2004, 2005). However, the key factor that led to relationship dissolution for both heterosexual and same-sex couples is an experience of decline in the quality of the relationship. In addition, similar to heterosexual couples, same-sex couples experience emotional distress as a result of relationship dissolution (Kurdek, 1997; Mohr, 2008). Despite the greater frequency of relationship dissolution, same-sex couples have romantic relationships that are sustainable and successful (Kurdek, 1995, 2004; Peplau and Spalding, 2000; Herek, 2006).

Aside from these limitations and concerns, speculations can be made regarding the experience of loss in same-sex couples as a method of extrapolation of the potential experience of divorce. Implications from an attachment perspective suggest that same-sex couples and heterosexual couples are similar in their experience of loss. Specifically, there is evidence that suggests there is not a difference in the way that same-sex and heterosexual couples experience distress as a result of loss (Kurdek, 1997; Mohr, 2008). Therefore, it is assumed that the attachment system acts in the same way for both same-sex and heterosexual couples.

There are many aspects of the identity development of same-sex individuals that have utility in the study of loss and attachment. Issues of stigma, prejudice, and oppression play an important role in the experience of same-sex individuals and most likely have an effect on the romantic relationships of them. Furthermore, the lack of extensive study in the area of same-sex couple development and attachment makes it difficult to fully understand their role in the romantic relationships of same-sex individuals. As noted above, there is victory in the ruling of the right to marry for same-sex individuals but, due to its recent implementation, there is not ample observation of same-sex marriages. To that end, there is also scarce study of marriage dissolutions of same-sex marriages.

Divorce in the Context of Immigration[1]

The occurrence of divorce in the setting of immigration has its own nuances and complexities. Some of the variables associated with immigration appear to increase the probability of divorce, while others seem to preclude it. Prominent among the former are the nonspecific stresses consequent upon immigration as well as the specific difficulties in marital life caused by immigration (e.g., differing rates of acculturation within the couple). Also, the more the motives for marrying pertain to warding off the pain and anxiety of immigration, the greater the threat to the continuity of marriage. Higher divorce rates in the immigrant's country of origin (e.g., Russia) also tend to be carried over. Prominent among the latter are low divorce rates in the country of origin (e.g., India, Italy), certain religious backgrounds (e.g., Catholic), and the extra-dependence immigrant partners have upon each other, and their extraordinary commitment to providing a secure home base for their children.

These speculative ideas are supported by empirical studies. A highly sophistical statistical survey, involving individuals from 31 countries who had migrated to Australia, found the overall divorce rate among immigrants to be lower than the mainstream Australian population (Khoo and Zhao, 2001). However, when the immigrant sample was broken down according to the country of origin, those from China, Thailand, Hungary, and the former USSR were revealed to have higher and those from India, Italy, Greece, and Sri Lanka lower divorce rates than the total Australian population. In the United States, immigrants from Mexico and other Latin American countries (Brooks, 2006; Chapman, 2007) and India (Dasgupta and Warrier, 1996) have lower divorce rates than the U.S. population at large. These studies support the idea that the divorce rate in an immigrant population is greatly affected by the prevalence of divorce in the immigrants' culture of origin. Whether the frequency of divorce in the immigrant population is higher or lower than the mainstream population, therefore, depends upon the correlation of the prevalence of divorce in the country of origin with the prevalence of divorce in the country of adoption. In the United States, where the modal divorce rate is sky high, the immigrant population invariably turn out to have a lower rate.

A multifactorial study of 12,076 immigrants to the United States from 24 different European countries (Furtado, Macén, and Sevilla-Sanz, 2009) found that when the divorce rate in the country of origin increases by one, the probability that an immigrant from that country in the United States is divorced increases by three percentage points. Thus, immigrants from Russia are 10 percentage points more likely to be divorced than immigrants from Italy. In effect, there was a robust correlation between home country divorce rates and divorce probability after immigration to the United States. Among other findings of this study were (i) immigrants from richer countries were less likely to divorce, (ii) the geographically carried-over effect of culture appeared more influential for women than men, and (iii) the impact of culture seemed greater for immigrants residing in homoethnic communities, suggesting that beliefs and attitudes are transmitted both vertically (from parents to children) and horizontally (from peer groups within the ethnic community).

Generally speaking, immigrants have similar reasons for seeking divorce (e.g., mutual unhappiness, lack of love, adultery) as do the natives. However, their exposure to stresses that are specific to immigration can compromise their capacity to satisfactorily handle the challenges of married life. Both subtle and dramatic factors play a role here. Prominent among the former is the development of an "acculturation gap" (Prathikanti, 1997) between the two partners, whereby one becomes more assimilated in the mainstream culture than the other. Prominent among the latter is an immigrant's "discovery" of his or her dormant homosexuality. Heterosexual escapades of married men with little sexual experience before arriving in a country with less rigid sexual mores can also lead to marital strife and result in divorce. Fascinatingly, the more entrenched and clandestine extramarital affairs (especially common among the Southeast Asian immigrants) often turn out to be less fatal for the marriage, even while causing a lot of pain to the betrayed partner. Such liaisons develop in order to avoid marital dissolution (while enjoying extramarital sexuality) in the first place.

Immigration can increase the power differential between the spouses, which, in turn, becomes a source of marital tension. Such power differential often results from one partner (frequently the man) being the sole wage earner and the other (almost invariably the woman) lacking proper papers ("green card" in the United States) for seeking legal protection and asserting civil rights. Dependency of such proportions renders women vulnerable to exploitation and abuse. While true for women brought to the West after primitively arranged marriages, this situation is even more applicable to "mail-order brides."[2] Many remain trapped in unhappy and suffocating marriages. Others break out and seek help from community shelters, which, thankfully, are growing in numbers.

Besides gender, the ethnicity of the marital partners also plays a role in assuring marital stability or contributing to marital breakdown. Data extracted from the 1990 U.S. Census suggests that heteroethnic marriages have a higher probability of divorce than homoethnic marriages (Kalmijn, 1993). However, such statistics are dubious. Calculating these statistics is difficult and open to all sorts of questions. Sung (1990) offers the example of four Chinese people, two of whom marry out of their group and the other two marry each other. Based upon the number of marriages, two of the three (66%) marriages are exogamous and one (33%) engodamous. But based upon the number of people involved, two (50%) have married exogamously and two (50%) endogamously. Divorce data calculated with the former baseline would of course differ from divorce data calculated with the latter as baseline. In her own study of Chinese exogamy in the United States, she found the divorce rate for heteroethnic Chinese marriages to be slightly higher. A reverse finding was reported by Wolf-Amansreh (1991) from Germany insofar as the divorce rate of heteroethnic German marriages was slighter lower. The difference did not reach a statistically significant level in either of these studies, however. This suggests that comparisons along the heteroethnic-homoethnic variable alone are not enough to reveal what sustains or unravels immigrant marriages. More subtle variables might be involved here. The fate of heteroethnic immigrant marriages seems to depend upon a large number of variables that extend far and beyond the intrapsychic economy of love and hate within the psyche of each partner and in the relational matrix of the couple. Culturally upheld roles, gender dynamics, economic factors, and the communal surround in which the couple resides also play a powerful role here.

Another important issue is whether factors contributing adversely to the outcome of divorce are more prevalent among immigrants. Immigrants often do not have a large number of significant family members in their adopted country to whom they can turn for solace as the distress of marital dissolution overwhelms them. Their post-divorced loneliness is thus compounded. For immigrant women of lower socioeconomic status, matters are even more complicated. They can seldom call on their families "back home" for support, not only because of distance and cost, but because often their families have a vested interest in keeping their daughters abroad and would lose face if they returned home (Breger, 1998; Abraham, 2000). The situation becomes worse if the married daughter was sending some money to the parents left behind and/or if she comes from a country where divorce is a rare and shocking event.

Children of divorced immigrant parents also suffer more because of the lack of uncles, aunts, cousins, and grandparents in their parents' adopted country. The loss of security that comes from an intact family is accentuated if the parental divorce results in the sale of the family residence. While it is often beyond the means of the divorcing couple, salvaging this last vestige of continuity might be of great help to the children and make their mourning process a little easier. Needless to add that the parents, themselves aggrieved and hurt, would need to make an extra effort to take care of their children (both jointly and separately), who have little access to other adult figures for support. Their feeling different from their peers might become more burdensome with the addition of the social shame of coming from a broken home. For children who belong to an ethnic group with markedly low divorce rate, finding homoethnic peers with similar familial backgrounds might be difficult; this can further increase their loneliness and depression. Yet another complicating factor is the exposure to the parents' post-divorce dating and romantic liaisons, for which immigrant children might be less prepared than their Western counterparts.

Divorce of Therapists and Analysts

Conducting psychotherapy and psychoanalysis requires a relatively peaceful mind that is the product of a relatively stable life. Our using the word "relatively" in this context is meant to indicate that no utopian model of stability and equanimity is being upheld here; therapists are no different as human beings from others and are equally vulnerable to the ordinary ups and downs of life. The "psychotherapeutic instrument" (Olinick, 1976) is capable of absorbing the tumult of daily life without becoming seriously compromised. However, crises of greater magnitude do affect the therapist's ability to carry on their work properly. This is amply evident in the literature dealing with the therapist's relocation (Aarons, 1975; Kaplan et al., 1994), pregnancy (Diamond, 1992; Stuart, 1997; Fallon and Brabender, 2003), illness (Schwartz and Silver, 1990; Friedman, 1991; Cristy, 2001), and aging (Tallmer, 1992; Eissler, 1993).

Far less attention has been paid to the therapist's divorce. Since many psychotherapists and psychoanalysts do get divorced, the paucity of writings in this realm is curious. In fact, to the best of our knowledge, only three papers on this topic (Schlachet, 1996; Shane, 2002; Basescu, 2009) exist in the entire psychoanalytic literature. Could it be that despite its prevalence and greater acceptance by society at large, divorce is still experienced as a deep personal failure by therapists and therefore felt difficult to report upon? Or is it the wish to protect patients from "over-stimulation" (by getting to know too many personal details about their therapist's life) that prevents therapists from writing about their own divorces?

We do not know. We do know what the three published papers and some informal conversations (with our divorced colleagues) tell us. Schlachet's (1996) contribution focuses upon the disruptive effect of divorce on the therapist's clinical equanimity. The feelings of shame and of being a failure can especially tax the therapist's sense of pride and efficacy; the burden of such affects can then lead to preoccupied states and vulnerability to counter-transference reactions. Faced with such crisis himself, Schlachet held on ever more tightly to the "trio of guideposts" (Pine, 1997) of anonymity, neutrality, and abstinence. At times, he acknowledged that *something* was going on with him but even then did not reveal the specifics; instead, he invited the patient to associate to what he or she imagined was going on. Schlachet admits that it required of him "the most resolute concentration, the most intense energy, even a certain amount of affective isolation, to continue the work in a reasonably balanced manner" (p. 146).

Shane's (2002) paper described the added pain that comes from being a partner in a well-known marital couple that has come apart; she and her husband, Morton Shane, were both prominent psychoanalysts. She describes the social outfall of her divorce in a painful but straightforward way:

> Several years ago my husband and I separated and then quickly divorced. Because we had been together for a long period of time, because we had virtually grown up together, had children together, worked together in psychoanalysis, studied together, wrote, published, taught and spoke at conferences together, and, finally, because ours was an unusually happy union, the shock created in our professional and personal worlds by our separation seemed enormous. The rumors, and then the confirming announcements themselves, were greeted with surprise, disbelief, and even rage. I think the rage was about having to give up an idealization of a prominent couple before they were ready to do so. People— colleagues, friends, patients, and supervisees—responded with dismay and with accusations. Some questioned whether we had been fraudulent in the presentation of ourselves; others felt we had been insufficiently protective of them. One supervisee asked plaintively, "Couldn't you have tried harder to work it out, for our sakes, at least?" People would confess their fears: "If it could happen to you, it could happen to anyone." (p. 581)

Moving on to the effects of her divorce on her ongoing clinical work, Shane has the following to say:

> For the majority of my patients, my separation and divorce brought change. For some patients it created hope, at least ultimately; with only one patient was the disruption such that he found it necessary to terminate with me, feeling that the gossip about me, which assailed him everywhere, was just too intrusive to allow for a good therapeutic experience. With most patients, however, the disruption and all that ensued enhanced our mutual implicit relational knowing, that is, in the wake of that disruption, more conscious and unconscious understanding about ourselves and one another evolved in the intersubjective context between us. I imagine the possibility that some patients remained in treatment out of loyalty or concern for me, but I feel, perhaps too optimistically, that most who stayed got something out of the change both in me and in our ways of being together, something that they may not have gotten in treatment with me had the change, with all its untoward, unpredicted, and unpredictable perturbational effects, not occurred. (pp. 582–583)

Shane offers four detailed clinical vignettes to highlight the impact of her divorce on the therapeutic process as it unfolded between her and her patient and as it resonated within her own psyche. She states that, like many other colleagues who underwent divorce, working clinically was "helpful, settling, and restorative" (p. 586) for her, even though a modicum of dissociation became mandatory under such circumstances. Taking up this last point, Shane bravely questions herself: "Did my conscious decision to dissociate all thoughts of the trouble in my marriage in order to focus upon my clinical work actually disguise what might be seen as a defensive, pathological dissociation, preserving thereby an outworn illusion of myself in marriage?" (p. 589). She acknowledges that she told some patients about her divorce and not others, basing such decisions on the intuitive grasp of each specific dyad's realities, attunements, and vulnerabilities. Shane concludes that "the question of whether to tell [patients] of the change in [one's] marital circumstance cannot be answered inevitably one way or the other; yes or no; no one standard criterion or technique can be applied to such decisions" (p. 598).

Seven years after Shane's thoughtful paper, Basescu (2009) published an essay on her own experience of divorce. She acknowledged that Shane's paper was gripping but felt that it lacked the reporting of the actual language Shane used to talk to her patients about what had happened. Basescu clearly values the importance of words, phrases, pauses, and intonations. She states:

> In my search for language to capture my own divorce experience, I often turned to poetic, literary, stream-of-consciousness writing. The feelings were so dense, intense, multi-layered, and complex that no linear, rational narrative voice could do the trick. Divorce is an experience of fragmentation, of shattering, and then of the reconstitution of one's life. In divorce, life is split apart, in ruins, and one has the opportunity, quite thrilling at times, to put it back together differently. My writing helped me to contain my ambivalence, to hold on to numerous layers of complex feeling at the same time. (p. 49)

Such "self-holding" allowed her to adopt a clinical approach that was "inevitably, different from Shane's and Schlachet's" (p. 58) and relied upon self-disclosure. However, such revelation was always followed by a return to the "customary" analytic stance of exploration and interpretation. Here's how she describes these developments.

> Some patients became aware of my divorce by noticing the disappearance of my wedding ring and asking about it. All eventually saw that I was moving. Many asked me why. Sometimes I asked for their fantasies first, but eventually I said, "My husband and I are divorcing and I am moving out of this building." Patients expressed shock, concern, sympathy, anxiety, curiosity, and other emotions. Sometimes in response to their concerns, I said, "I'm okay." This was a lie and not a lie. To the extent I was lying to them, I was also lying to myself. Although sometimes I thought I am saying I am okay but I'm not really okay, but I must be okay because here I am working and I couldn't be working if I weren't okay ... A few patients fired many questions at me: "why are you getting divorced? Did you initiate it? Are you having an affair? Are you dating? Are you a lesbian?

Are you going on vacation with just your children or with a new partner? Are you depressed?" I said: "It's been a long process, not sudden. I can't tell you all the details. It's extremely complicated. No one is the victimizer or the victimized" ... With everyone I said, "Tell me what you're feeling." Then we would go on, exploring their thoughts, reactions, and associations. And, I would be grateful to feel myself going-on-being using myself in this familiar way, when so much else in my life was shocking and unfamiliar. (pp. 58–59)

At times, Basescu had to stop a session because of her own pain becoming too large to contain. Doing so might appear to disturb the "letter" of the analytic frame but maintained its "spirit." Basescu adds an interesting observation that many of her patients became aware of her changed marital situation in their dreams before becoming cognizant of it in their waking associations.

All in all, this limited but poignant and instructive literature (Schlachet, 1996; Shane, 2002; Basescu, 2009) tells us that divorce of therapists (i) is as traumatic as anyone else's divorce, (ii) poses a challenge for the therapists' clinical functioning, (iii) is noticed directly or indirectly by their patients, and (iv) requires a nuance way of handling, which combines varying extent of self-disclosure, judicious modifications of the frame, validation of patients' perceptions, and, to the extent possible, maintenance of analytic technique in its proper sense.

"GOOD-ENOUGH" DIVORCE

Three conclusions can be safely drawn from the forgoing survey of literature: (i) divorce has powerful emotional antecedents and equally strong emotional consequences, (ii) most such consequences are adverse, and (iii) the negative impact of divorce lingers for a long time and involves not just the "primary" parties (i.e., marital partners and their offspring) but an ever increasing circle of affectively invested others. Given this somber picture and well aware of the high prevalence of divorce, one wonders if there is any way the damage can be minimized, the bloodshed controlled.

Extrapolating the prefix "good-enough" from Winnicott's (1960) celebrated concept of the "good-enough mother," one might search for the nosological boundaries of a "good-enough divorce." The pursuit yields the following five criteria:

- The decision to file for divorce should have been preceded much thoughtfulness and attempts to resolve the marital impasse by couples therapy.
- The primary goal of the two partners entering the divorce proceedings should be to separate from each other in a time-efficient manner;

destructive and narcissistic aims must be set aside in the service of a quick termination of marriage.

- Children should be protected and not used as strategic pawns, protective shields, or means for blackmail.
- A modicum of civility must be maintained during the proceedings and the partners must resist deploying "below-the-belt" rhetoric.
- After the divorce proceedings are over, and if realities (e.g., child-custody, graduation and marriage of children) dictate that the partners remain in contact with each other, all effort should be made to maintain good manners and basic cordiality.
- As months and years pass, deeper self-reflection upon one's erstwhile coupleship should set in, pushing each partner from their former "paranoid" and "manic" narrative to a changed, "depressive" narrative that allows the role of one's own blemishes and aggression in the failure of one's marriage.
- Finally, the divorce should lead neither to a quick "rebound" marriage nor to a life-long aversion to marriage.

This list of criteria can be criticized as not reflecting a "good-enough" divorce but an "ideal" divorce. Perhaps, that is true. And, therefore, an important "softening" caveat needs to be entered here. This declares that a divorce is to be regarded "good-enough" if most of the above-mentioned criteria are mostly met, most of the time, and to most extent. *That* seems a "good-enough" definition of a "good-enough" divorce!

CONCLUDING REMARKS

In this chapter, we have offered a broad survey of psychodynamic observations on the antecedents and consequences of divorce. Fully aware that divorce is a legal and not psychodynamic concept, we have explored the "emotional divorce" that invariably precedes the one granted by a court and have focused upon the emotional impact of the "actual" divorce upon the spouses, children (if any involved), and surrounding others. In doing so, we have taken into account both short-term and long-term sequelae of divorce, noting that often these reverberate for the remaining lifetime of the spouses and can be transgenerationally transmitted even to their children's offspring. We have also addressed the vicissitudes of divorce in three specific populations, namely, same-sex couples, immigrants, and therapists. We have then delineated the concept of a "good-enough divorce," giving voice to our belief that the adverse effects of divorce can be kept at a minimum, the process itself can take place in a civilized manner, and post-divorce self-reflection can temper the paranoid attitudes customarily associated with the occurrence.

One last point still needs to be made. This pertains to the occasional, unsung benefits of divorce for not only the erstwhile marital partners but for their children as well. This possibility is clear when the divorce has been precipitated by a partner's overt cruelty, serious substance abuse, and violence. The healthier, if co-dependent, partner and children can then carry on a less rocky and traumatizing existence. A gain of this sort is further consolidated if the spouse who stays with the children finds a better, more supportive partner. As children adapt to their new circumstances, their emotional turmoil settles and in fact, they display less distress symptoms than children living in high-conflict non-divorced families (Hetherington and Stanley-Hagan, 1999).

For spouses, too, divorce can propel psychic development, especially in the realm of adulthood versions of separation-individuation (Cantor, 1982; Rosbrow-Reich, 1988). The failure of marriages that were intended as an escape from merged relationships with primary objects or as a search for a "transformational object" (Bollas, 1979) can mobilize the much needed soul-searching. This might result in enhanced capacity for autonomy and separateness as well as a renunciation of the "ideal spouse representation" (Colarusso, 1997). The post-divorce period of solitude and contemplation, if not aborted by the hurry inherent in manic defences, can yield deeper insights into the self, greater tolerance of one's own limitations, and a less painful acceptance of blemishes in a future partner. These psychic advances can lay the groundwork for contentment and mutuality than has hitherto not been achievable in a relationship.

NOTES

1. Significant portions of this subsection have been taken from the senior author's book, *Immigration and Acculturation* (Akhtar, 2011), with permission from the author and from the book's publisher.

2. For the impact of "mail-order bride" industry (comprising of over 200 agencies) upon U.S. immigration, see Schole and Phataralaoha (2000).

Chapter Two

Divorce Is Not Good for Children and Other Living Things

Martin A. Silverman

As many as half of all marriages end in divorce. At times, this might be a good thing for a man and a woman who are unhappy together. At other times, it might be just one detail in the lives of people who are destined to be miserable with or without each other. In such an instance, leaving one another at least offers some hope of finding a better union, even if it is unlikely that it actually will be found. In either event, what if the couple dissolving the marriage has children? It is not very often that *they* want their parents to split up. What is the effect on *them* of their parents' marriage dissolving and the family structure crumbling? Children cannot help but be adversely affected by their world being fractured and fragmented. A sense of safety and security comes in large measure from feeling loved and protected by devoted parents who can be relied upon to be there to provide for their children's physical and emotional needs. And if their parents show themselves to be incapable of uniting together to handle life's challenges and of ironing out the inevitable wrinkles that develop in a relationship between two people, that hardly inspires the children take on the risks involved in entering into a trusting relationship with another person. In the course of their twenty-five-year, longitudinal study of children of divorce, Wallerstein, Lewis, and Blakeslee (2000) found that, as adults, children of separation and divorce tend far more frequently than children who grow up in intact families to hesitate about entering into relationships and to have difficulty remaining in them when they do so.

What is the impact, furthermore, on the children's self-image, self-esteem, and self-confidence? Prior to the acquisition of mature, hypothetico-deductive, abstract operational thinking in adolescence, children are very self-oriented and are limited in their capacity to grasp the full complexity of human functioning and interaction. If their parents have been defeated in their efforts to make a go of a marriage, it is almost inevitable that children will be inclined to blame themselves for it. If they had been better children who were able to make their parents happy, this never would have happened. It *must* be their fault. Children *need* parents! If they don't have them, they will invent them if they have to. The World War II Jewish children at the Hampstead Nursery who had been ransomed out of Nazi Europe but had lost their entire families demonstrated this dramatically. As they entered the successive phases of their developmental progression, they tended to *invent* the parents they needed to negotiate those forward steps, even telling tall tales about them, to fill the void. Children desperately need parents. As Edith Jacobson (1965) pointed out many years ago, children find it extremely difficult to admit that their parents have failed them. They need to idealize their parents and to be hopeful that their parents will be there for them, despite all evidence to the contrary. If they were to blame their parents, they would feel helpless and hopeless. When they take the blame onto themselves, there is always the hope that they—themselves—can become better and thereby win their parents' love and devotion. Their parents' job is to love, protect, and take care of them. Their job is to make their parents happy.

Even for adolescents, parental divorce presents a great deal of difficulty. Adolescence is a time of great change, a great deal of stress, and major challenges. Fonagy (2002), paradoxically, in fact, speculates that the very advent of abstract operational thinking presents adolescents with problems at the same time that it provides an intellectual tool for mastery, in that teenagers are more able than they were earlier in life to recognize how complex the world is and with how much they will have to contend as adults. They need all the help they can get. Daniel Offer and Melvin Sabshin (1966), in an important, normative study of adolescence, found that the group that sailed through adolescence swimmingly was the one that contained teenagers with families that not only were intact but had been solidly secure for several generations. People need to be enveloped by a sense of stability and reliability—and this is especially so for young people.

ALL DIVORCES ARE NOT THE SAME

As far as the children are concerned, not all divorces have the same impact. I had reason one day to call a family court judge with whom I needed to discuss something. I noticed that he didn't sound as jaunty as he usually sounded when we spoke. "You seem a little down," I said to him. "Did you have to have another root canal?" "No, it's not that," he said, after thanking me for remembering his recent, terrible dental experience and caring about how he was feeling. "It's this job! I hate it! I can't wait to get off this bench." (At that time in New Jersey, judges rotated periodically from one bench to another.)

He went on to say to me that he dealt with roughly three types of divorce. In one, two people decide that they have made a mistake. They shake hands and part amicably. When children are involved, the impact on them usually is manageable. That happens, he said, no more than 10% of the time. Far more often, there is a lot of ongoing contention and anger between the parents. This kind of divorce tends to be very hard on the children, but more often than not he is able to get across to the parents that they need to tone things down for the children's sake. It doesn't eliminate the damage being done to the children, but at least it reduces it. About 60% of the divorces coming before him, he said, were of this type.

It was the third group that was getting him down. This is the kind of divorce, he said, that is all-out war—before, during, and after the divorce. "And the children," he emphasized, "are the civilian casualties!" They made up about 30% of the divorces, he said, but they took up 90% of his time—and he absolutely hated it. It is this kind of divorce that led me to modify the antinuclear war slogan of the 1950s and 1960s—"War is not good for children and other living things"—to construct the title I chose for this presentation.

What the judge said to me that day was amply confirmed by what Wallerstein, Lewis, and Blakeslee[1] found in their long-range study of the effect of divorce on children. When the children who were the civilian casualties of this third type of divorce grew up, they were far more likely than those who had experienced more civil dissolutions of their parents' marriages to have trouble down the line. The incidence of clinical anxiety disorder and depression was far higher in this group than in grownup survivors of less volatile family disruption. Far more of them experienced a contentious divorce themselves when they grew up. Many more of them had difficulty maintaining stable relationships, and a good number were wary of even taking a chance on entering into a relationship with another person. After all, they knew all too well what had happened in their parents' relationship!

One of the most devastating scenarios, in my experience, is the one in which parental divorce leads to loss of a parent, either because of abandonment or because one parent, usually the mother, demonizes the other parent and blocks him from having access to the children. And what is the effect on a child of supervised visitation with one of the parents? I do a good many psychiatric evaluations as a part of Child Study Team assessments of children who are having academic and behavioral difficulties in school. The most common situation by far which I encounter is one that involves a child with an attention deficit hyperactivity disorder, often with related learning disabilities, who also has very largely or totally lost contact with his or her father (or mother, although this occurs much less often) as aftermath of parental divorce. This is an extremely difficult combination for children to experience. Sometimes it is because the father has broken off contact, not only with the child's mother but also with the child. He may even have moved far away. At other times, the child's mother has blocked the father from having contact with the child after a nasty custody battle via threats, a restraining order, and/or a contentious child support battle. John Irving has written a series of moving and disturbing novels that center about abandonment, loneliness, the pain of not having a father, and the wistful yearning for a loving family and an intact, stable home. His parents divorced before he was born, and his father totally abandoned him. His mother remarried when he was six years of age, but the absence of a father until then had enormous impact upon him. As Mel Gussow reported in the *New York Times* in 1998, it was not until Irving had grown up and his own first marriage had dissolved that he learned, from some things his mother gave him at that point in time, that his father had been a war hero. He wove that into his next novel, *The Cider House Rules*, incorporating it into the persona of one of the important characters he created for the book. Gussow observed that

> running through John Irving's novels is the theme of lost children and absent parents, from the unknown father in *The World According to Garp* to *The Cider House Rules* in which "all the parents are missing." [A pivotal line, in Irving's newest book at that time, *A Widow for One Year*, reads,] "The grief of lost children never dies." (Gussow, 1998, p. E1)

KEY DETERMINANTS OF THE IMPACT
OF DIVORCE ON CHILDREN

This brings me to (1) the importance of the age and level of development of a child at the time of the parental divorce as determinants of the effect the divorce has upon the child and (2) the significance of what is going on in each parent (each of whom brings the residues of his or her own childhood experience) before, during, and following the split. In certain ways, the younger the child at the time, the greater is the impact likely to be. Attachment and emotional object constancy, in the best of circumstances, are never as firm and total as would be optimal. The strength and stability of attachment are subject to the vagaries of the child's particular temperament in interaction with the variable and shifting empathy and attunement of the parenting person. The impact of parental divorce upon children is determined in large part by their level of emotional and cognitive development at the time it occurs. The effect upon each child depends to a great extent upon how much development has already taken place to prepare the child for comprehending, processing, and dealing with what is occurring in the child's life. There also is variability in the extent to which children's attachment with each parent prior to the dissolution of their parents' marriage has become solid enough to enable them to hold on to their connectedness with their parents during wartime and its aftermath.

Nothing, furthermore, occurs in a vacuum. Children who already have other problems, such as an attention deficit disorder, learning disabilities, or other interferences with self-image, self-esteem, and the ability to manage independently and autonomously, inevitably will be more seriously affected by parental divorce than those who are fortunate enough to be relatively hale and hearty. What each parent experienced in his or her own childhood, including whether a parental divorce was a part of it, further influences the way in which that parent speaks and acts with regard to the divorce and the custody issues that unfold. A parent who went through a fractious parental divorce in his or her own childhood is often likely to repeat the very things that troubled that parent the first time around. A parent who harbors extreme resentment of and anger toward the other parent is likely to view and speak about him or her in ways that create problems for the children. Not all parents, furthermore, are equally capable of freeing themselves from being preoccupied with their own narcissistic injury and narcissistic rage over what is taking place to tune in and respond helpfully to what their children are experiencing.[2] The intensity of one parent's animosity toward the other *often* interferes with the ability to be attuned to the impact upon the *children* of what is taking place between the parents.

Clinical vignette: 1

I recall, for example, a four-year-old boy I treated some time ago whose parents had gone through an extremely nasty divorce and were now engaged in a battle over custody and visitation that was nothing short of all-out war. He was sitting on the floor one day constructing a town out of construction paper and crayons (my thoughts involved "making a new and better world for himself?" and "using cry-ons?"). As he worked, he told me about the latest battle that was going on between his parents, in which he was the tug-of-war rope that stretched between them. The latest issue involved his mother's wish to have the court change Adam's surname from his father's last name to her maiden name, to which she had reverted after the divorce. As intended, this absolutely infuriated my little patient's father. He grew angrier and angrier as he spoke with me about it. I cannot forget the hatred in his eyes and the look of fury that crept over his face, as he looked up at me and said: "Someday, I'm going to grow up—and then I'm going to change my name to *neither of their names!*"

THE IMPACT OF DIVORCE AND SEPARATION ON VERY YOUNG CHILDREN

In a recent presentation during the annual meeting of the American Psychoanalytic Association, Linda Gunsberg (2016) described her observations of infants and toddlers who were shuttled back and forth between their mothers' and their fathers' homes, as decreed by a judge who was concerned with the rights of each parent. Especially when these very young children were removed periodically from their mothers' care to spend increasing periods of time at their fathers' homes, they showed increasing signs of emotional distress. They exhibited vigilant attention to indications that they were about to be picked up and taken away, such as seeing their mother drawing the curtains or closing the blinds in their rooms, with observable anxiety. They became visibly distressed, and they objected strongly to being taken out of their cribs or out of their bedrooms. The children being shuttled back and forth from between one parent's home and that of the other very often developed a sleep disturbance in which they woke up repeatedly, apparently to make sure that their mother was still there. They also tended to become so clingy to mommy that they shadowed her, including when she left them just for a few minutes to use the bathroom. They often tended to lose developmental gains they already had made. Some reverted, for example, from walking to crawling.

When they returned to their mother's home after spending time with their father, they tended to check to make sure that all their toys and cherished possessions were still there. *Loss breeds fear of further loss.* Something similar often occurs with older children whose parents have split up, that is, they become overanxious at times when their mother is ill or if they cannot quickly find her when they want or need something from her. It is no mere coincidence that this is similar to what can be observed after one of a child's parents has died!

The infants and toddlers whom Gunsberg observed not infrequently tended to scream and bite their mother on the shoulder or breast after returning from an overnight with their father or especially, from a stay of several days with him. They also tended to retreat into such self-soothing behaviors as hugging a blanket and carrying it around, rubbing their genitals against something, or, in the case of girls, inserting things into their vaginas. Some of them withdrew emotionally or withdrew from their mothers. Some even retreated behind blank stares. With advancing age, children are increasingly able to understand and to deal with parental divorce, especially if their parents are able to more or less set aside their differences with each other and work together in relative harmony in caring for the children, but it is never truly easy for them.

Divorce, especially when it is contentious and involves abandonment by or failure of the secondary parent to satisfy the needs of the primary parent, can interfere seriously with the primary parent's ability to be there emotionally for the child. When one of the parents is consumed with rage at the other one, that is very likely to spill over into complaining about and bad-mouthing the other parent, as well as interfering with the ability to think empathically about the effect of this upon the child and to even think about the child's sensibilities and needs. Imagine what it is like when *both* parents are enraged at each other! Divorce and its consequences, similarly, can heighten the child's otherwise ordinary ambivalence toward their parents, which interferes with the development of secure, healthy attachment and of solid, healthy self-esteem. Even when a caring, devoted replacement father enters the scene, it can be very difficult for the child to accept the newcomer. Stepparents are not always enough to salve the wound of abandonment by the original one (Silverman, 2001). It can also be extremely difficult for a child to deal with the rage that is mobilized toward an abandoning parent, as Edith Jacobson (1965) has observed, so the rage is directed instead against the parent *who is there,* increasing the level of ambivalence toward that parent as well.

SOME CLINICAL EXAMPLES OF THE PROBLEMS EXPERIENCED BY CHILDREN OF DIVORCE

Let me share a clinical experience that exemplifies this. I have treated a number of children, as well as adults, who were or had been the "civilian casualties" of the war between parents who are going through an extremely contentious divorce process.

Clinical vignette: 2

Ten-year-old Billy came to me while his parents were engaged in an extremely angry, bitterly contested divorce and custody battle. A friend of the family who was in analysis with me, and whose problems stemmed in part from the impact upon *him* of a nasty parental divorce during his own childhood, had urged them to get help for him as soon as possible. The relationship between Billy's parents had been steadily deteriorating for many years before his father left Billy's mother to start a new life with another woman, with whom he had been involved for some time. Nasty legal proceedings had begun a couple of years ago and had recently come to a conclusion. Billy was explosively eruptive, breaking things, kicking holes in the wall of his bedroom, and even hurling a chair through a window during an argument with his mother. He treated his younger sibling abominably. His misbehavior occurred at home, but not when he went to his father's new house, although his coldness toward his father and refusal to accept the new woman in his father's life or relate to her children saddened them. His school performance had declined to the point of his being in danger of having to repeat the year.

Billy brought his hurt and anger right into the treatment situation. He came for sessions under protest, at least on the surface, and at first he refused to talk to me about what he was experiencing. When I expressed compassion for what he must have been going through instead of criticizing him for his misbehavior as he had expected me to do, his demeanor softened and he began to tell me about his unhappiness. He spewed out angry complaints about his mother, which, as we eventually came to see, in significant ways mirrored his father's complaints about her. He rationalized his explosively aggressive behavior toward his mother and his sister as justified by how they made *him* feel. It was very difficult for him, for quite some time, to recognize how angry he also was at his father. It became clear that he needed his father much too much and was far too enraged at him for having left for Billy to be able to admit to himself how hurt he felt by his father abandoning him, his mother, and his sister to join another family. Slowly and carefully, partly via calling attention to the way in which he was transferring his anger at his parents onto me, I helped him recognize the extent to which he was displacing his rage at his father onto his mother and to which he was taking out his resentment of his father's new (step)children on his sister. I proceeded, also carefully, to help each of his parents grasp the meaning of Billy's misbehavior. This eventually led to their backing away from each blaming the other one when they spoke to Billy and to their becoming more empathically tuned in to what Billy was going through that was being expressed in the way he was behaving.

Billy's explosive wildness at the home of his mother, the primary parent with whom he spent most of his time, gradually decreased, as did his violent behavior toward her (his sister had to wait a lot longer). He began instead to become critical and angry toward me, especially when he perceived me as failing to accurately understand what he was feeling toward me or as being more devoted to other patients and more interested in their needs than in his. As we explored the transferential aspects of this, he became more and more able to express his hurt and anger at his father for what he perceived as his having betrayed him in a more direct fashion when he was with his father—who had made good use by then of the sessions I had with him and had become much more tolerant of Billy's negative feelings toward him. It took a lot of work and a fair amount of time, but Billy eventually developed a good relationship not only with each of his parents but also with his sister and his new stepsiblings. Along the way, his performance in school greatly improved, partly because we were able to discover and deal effectively with a mild attention deficit disorder, the existence of which had been adumbrated and obscured by the extreme emotional reaction he had been having to his parents' separation and divorce. Billy has continued to keep in touch with me as a valued friend and ally. He did very well in college and is flourishing in jobs that are in the same area in which his father worked while Billy was growing up. He has his own apartment, at a distance from but not very far from where his parents live. He has a valued group of friends and has had a series of girlfriends, but he has not yet developed a deep relationship with any of them. That just might take a bit more work.

I have commented on the tendency of children of separation and divorce to blame themselves for the breakup of their parents' marriage. This stems in part from young children's cognitive immaturity and concentration upon themselves. An additional source often involves the triangular, oedipal conflicts which children generally develop in the course of their development.

Clinical vignette: 3

Eleven-year-old Chip, for example, was brought for assistance because of extremely oppositional, hostile, aggressive behavior toward his mother which at times frightened her. He punched, kicked, and threw things at her, and very recently had threatened her with a kitchen knife. His parents had gone through a divorce a year or so earlier that was unpleasant, especially for Chip's mother, but it was relatively civil (at least on the surface). They did not battle with one another, although Chip's mother was quite irked that his father did not punish him or otherwise manage to stop him from treating her so terribly. His mother was the primary parent, but his father lived close by and Chip's parents were quite cooperative and flexible with each other with regard to the visitation agreement. Chip had friends, did well at school, and enjoyed a number of hobbies and sports activities. It was only at home, with his mother, that he was a terror.

Chip at first objected to coming for treatment, but only infrequently did he actually refuse to come for a session. He tended to be sullen and distant at first but gradually became more responsive and verbal. What emerged was that he *had to* fight with his mother and that he *had to* fight off any closeness with her. It was not only that he identified with his father in blaming her for his unhappiness, and that he that he focused the anger he felt toward *both* of his parents solely on his mother, the one who did *not* leave. An even more significant determinant of his behavior, as gradually became clear to us, was that he had experienced his parents' splitting up as an oedipal victory that terrified him and filled with him with so much guilt that he had to repeatedly draw down punishment upon himself.

His sexual excitement revealed itself both in his inability to allow himself *any form of* pleasurable interaction with his mother whatsoever and in his allowing me to observe that his teasing and punching his younger sister in the waiting room evolved at times into very sensuous rolling around on the floor with her and at times making coital movements after he had wrestled her down and gotten on top of her. As he eventually became able to verbalize, more or less directly, it was extremely difficult for him to find himself replacing his father as the man of the house in which he lived with his mother and sister. The excitement it engendered, undiluted and unchecked, in the absence of a father at home with them, who could serve as a containing and controlling influence, was simply too much for him. His mother periodically complained to me that his father was afraid of Chip being angry at him for having left the family and therefore was reluctant to punish Chip when he mistreated his mother. Eventually, Chip made it clear that it troubled *him* even more than it did his mother. We eventually became able to talk together about how wishing for a victory over one's father and actually achieving it are very different indeed. No one truly enjoys having competition get out of control like that.

Even when their parents have gone through a divorce (and one or both of them have remarried) but have decided to live relatively close to one another for the children's sake, the arrangements still can present difficulties for the children. Not being in the same neighborhood all the time can make it difficult to interact with friends the way a child who lives in one home all the time can do. Going back and forth between two houses interferes with being there reliably for one's friends. Being in one house and needing but not having something the child needs because it is in the other house can be very distressing at times. Of course, the most important thing the child needs but does not have is the other parent. It can be especially difficult when one or the other parent remarries and has a child or two with the new spouse. A youngster with whom I worked some time ago sadly said to me: "My parents tell me that I'm lucky to have two homes. They don't understand that when I go back and forth between two houses, I feel like a visitor in each of them. I feel like I have *no* home!"

STEPCHILDREN AND STEPPARENTS

This brings me to the challenges faced by children whose parents remarry after a divorce. Even when stepparents are not only loving and devoted to them but are relatively well attuned to what their stepchildren are going through, it is not necessarily easy for either of them to establish the kind of relationship which they want to have with one another. To accept a new parent in place of a former, one can create an insoluble loyalty conflict. It can also be very difficult for a stepparent to step into the place that used to be occupied by the original parent, especially when the child feels more or less abandoned by that parent. The anger experienced by a child who feels that he or she has been abandoned tends to be transferred on to the stepparent, that is, to the one *who is there*. How dare this intruder presume to replace the original parent? Is the child supposed to give up the idealization that has had to be maintained toward the one who was lost? Is he or she trying to make the child lose hope of someday being reunited with the lost parent? In addition to this, for some period of time, the child has had the remaining parent to her or himself. That too is going to be taken away now!?!

Clinical vignette: 4

I met Diane when she was in her late thirties. She was a beautiful woman and had a husband who adored her and provided very well for her. She had two beautiful children, a lovely home, and a large circle of friends. Despite all this, she was extremely unhappy, had little or no confidence in herself, and lived in constant fear that her friends didn't really care about her and would abandon her at any moment. She attached herself to a succession of women whom she idealized and whom she slavishly followed as her guide and mentor in all things. Her love for her husband was marred by her envy of his accomplishments, his self-confidence, and his pleasure in showing off his abilities and his material possessions, while she viewed herself as unintelligent and unaccomplished and wanted to hide from the world. Her looks were the only thing that gave her any reason to feel good about herself, and she dreaded growing old and losing them.

Diane's parents were divorced less than a year after she was born. She was told that she had had visits with her father periodically until she was two but, according to her mother, she was always unhappy during and after her visitations with him. When she was two, her mother stopped the visitations and even blocked her paternal grandparents from visiting her, so that, as she sadly told me, she had no family except her mother until her mother remarried when she was six years old. Her father, furthermore, reportedly made no objection to being prevented from seeing her. According to her mother, in fact, he was sorry that she had been born as a girl rather than as a boy. Her mother depicted him to her as an extremely good-looking but extremely vain and self-centered man who did not care about anyone but himself. It troubled Diane that she had no direct recollection of what he looked like. She never even saw a picture of him, in fact, until her mother finally gave her a couple of photographs of him when she already had become an adult. Even then, she was unsure whether she resembled her father or her mother. To make things worse, her father died before she was six, so that all hope of ever being reunited with him completely evaporated. At first, Diane told me that she knew "intellectually" that she should have felt "devastated" at being "rejected and abandoned" by her father, but that she did not feel it because "that's only an abstract rejection and I don't have a face to attach to it."

Her mother's second marriage was to a man who not only was very kind and loving to her mother but to Diane as well. He legally adopted her and raised her as his own. He provided well for her and was eager to teach her things and help her with her homework. She regularly shrank away from him, however, and she assiduously rejected his offers of assistance with her schoolwork, so much so that she was totally unable to learn anything from him, even though she had such severe attention and learning problems that school for her was a source of misery rather than mastery. Diane vacillated between describing herself as pushing away from his ministrations and describing him as undemonstrative (or was it that he eventually gave up in response to her continually recoiling from his shows of affection for her?). She always felt uncomfortable in his presence and regretted that her mother had married him—at the same time that she cringed and felt miserable any time they quarreled.

Diane was an extremely unhappy girl who dreaded going to school and dreaded returning home from school. In her unhappiness, she sought solace in food. The food she carried with her to serve as her lunch arrived at school inside of her rather than in the container in which it had started the journey. She always ate it all on the way. She became quite overweight, which robbed her of the beauty that had been her one source of feeling good about herself. We gradually became aware together that her overeating was multi-determined. It not only resulted from her need to comfort herself in response to her unhappiness and misery, but it also served to obliterate the good looks that connected her with her lost father and to make herself unattractive to the stepfather whose interest in her and shows of affection toward her made her uncomfortable. As an adult, she wrestled constantly against the pull to either overeat or over-shop. She struggled mightily, and more or less successfully, to control her weight through diet and exercise, but the childhood gorging morphed into masochistically taking very poor care of her teeth and gums so she suffered from frequent, painful dental problems. As an adult, she also dissolved into fits of sobbing whenever she saw a television commercial involving or read about either a happy family or a happy mother–daughter relationship.

Diane slimmed down in adolescence and became a very attractive young lady. One day, when she was a high school student, the sight of her in a bathing suit at the beach entranced a good-looking young man who instantly fell head over heels for her. He eventually became her husband, but this evolved in a very interesting way. She was overjoyed that he "liked, admired, wanted, and took pleasure" in her. He became the "love of (her) life!" She adored him! When he went off to college, however, he broke off their relationship, partly because he found himself overwhelmed both by her emotionality and by the intensity of her hunger for closeness. She was devastated, but she would not give up. She kept reaching out and making contact with him in one way or another.

She had no problem attracting young men, and soon she was dating someone who was heading toward the same profession as her stepfather. She skillfully arranged for him and her previous boyfriend to learn about each other. Then she played one against the other—until the first boyfriend finally told her to send the new one packing. They went steady for a while, after which she *broke off with him*! After a series of breakups and reunions, in which she tested his loyalty to her and his devotion to her, he finally proposed and they got married. To complete the tale of repetition of the past in the present, later on in life she ran into the man who had been her "new and other" boyfriend in the triangular interaction she had engineered. To her surprise, she found herself feeling just as uncomfortable in his presence as she had felt in her stepfather's presence many years earlier.

The marriage was a happy one, although she very much envied the close relationship her husband had with his mother, and felt guilty when she found *herself* moving toward good relations with her. It felt to her like betraying her own mother, whom she showered with attention and presents even as she resented her mother's "vanity and selfishness" (the very faults her mother had attributed toward her biological father) and she boiled inside with anger which she could not let herself express. At first, Diane connected her anger at her mother to the sense of entitlement she exhibited toward Diane. She gradually realized, however, that far more important was her rage at her mother for depriving her of a relationship with the father whom she never had ceased idealizing and who, unconsciously, she had never ceased hoping would return to her. She remembered that her mother, when she was angry at Diane, periodically blamed *her* for the breakup of the marriage—because her father had not wanted a child at that time. It took a great deal of work to help Diane sort out all of this so that she might disentangle the past and the present.

If the original parent truly has abandoned a child and the remaining parent seriously badmouths the lost parent and interferes with contact with that parent, with transfer of his or her anger at the former spouse on to the child that represents a connection with her or him, the situation can be very bad indeed. Not every stepparent, furthermore, is able to realize that actually it is the lost, abandoning parent at whom the child is angry. When the stepparent misreads the hostility or the pushing away, the child exhibits to him or her as intolerable ingratitude, insult, and rejection and responds in kind, it can be difficult or impossible to develop a comfortable relationship with the child.

THE LONG-TERM EFFECTS UPON CHILDREN OF SEPARATION AND DIVORCE

What happens early in life tends to influence development from that point onward and to be carried forward into adulthood, when it can reappear after having lain dormant, in the form of disturbance of various aspects of functioning or repetition (at times in disguised form) of what had been experienced in the distant past. The degree to which children weather the impact upon them of parental divorce and/or recover from it varies widely, depending upon their elasticity, adaptability, and innate emotional strengths as well as upon the degree to which their parents, other adults in their lives, and their siblings are able to help them do. Success in this regard does not always come easily.

Clinical vignette: 5

Eddie, for example, came to me for assistance because he was engaging compulsively in activities that threatened the stability of his marriage to a wonderful woman whom he loved very much. He was terrified that if his wife lost patience with him and divorced him, it could have a devastating effect on his baby daughter, who was the love of his life. His parents had divorced when *he* was a baby, less than a year of age. It was an extremely stormy divorce, and things continued to be stormy between them even afterward. He saw his father bi-weekly, in supervised visitations. He and his mother moved in with his mother's mother, who turned out to be the only person in his life with whom he has ever had a mutually loving relationship and who eventually turned out to be a stabilizing, life-saving force for him. His relationship with his mother was disappointing and volatile, and it remained so after she remarried when Eddie was seven or eight years old and they moved to another state. His stepfather was kind enough, but Eddie never was able to feel close to him—or to the half-brother who was born a few years after his mother's remarriage. His father and his stepfather bitterly disliked one another, and they fought repeatedly. Eddie had horrible memories of the worst of those fights.

Eddie never was able to feel close to any of his classmates at school either. He always felt like an inferior person and like a social outsider in school. Although intelligent, he never felt good about himself or had confidence in his abilities, and he was an indifferent student who did not do his work, failed some of his classes, and finally dropped out of school when he was sixteen or seventeen—which also was when his father remarried (only to go through a second divorce half a dozen years later). He went through a series of desultory jobs for a while and then returned to school after his grandmother implored him do so. He went on to college only to drop out once again a little while later. He moved back to where his mother and stepfather were living and went to work with his stepfather. He did very well until the market crash that followed the bursting of the subprime mortgage bubble wiped him out.

When he moved back to living with his grandmother, his whole life turned around. She devoted herself to building his belief in himself and his value, and she *insisted* that he go back to school and work hard there. He attended a community college, where he also discovered that, contrary to his expectations, lots of girls were attracted to him. He went out with one girl after another, but once they became intimate and were hurtling toward a truly meaningful relationship he would break it off and move on to another girl whom he could excite and then disappoint. He did very well at the community college and then did so well at a four-year college and in graduate school that he landed a very well-paying job at a big company, where he was advancing rapidly at the time he came to see me.

Eddie told me that he always sought his father's approval—at the same time that he attempted to prove that he could do very well without him. When he was achieving success in his stepfather's business, his father asked him to help him invest in that area. Somehow, that turned out to be a big flop, and his father lost his money. His father was extremely angry, and they did not speak to one another again for six or seven years. It was only after Eddie's baby daughter was born and Eddie reached out to him at that time that communication between them was restored.

Eddie told me something that is very significant. It was not just with women that he avoided closeness, but with everyone! He had no friends, he said, except his wife, who was a remarkably calm and even-tempered person who put up with his quirks and with his moods—in marked contrast to his mother, who was an impatient, easily frustrated, explosively eruptive woman while he was growing up with her. Things progressed very rapidly after they met, and they got married just three months later, before he had a chance to push her away. (I doubt that it is mere coincidence that she too is the product of a terrible divorce between her parents that continues to be a source of great pain for her.) Even with his little daughter, who was just a few months old, he was frightened because he "did not feel an all-encompassing, unbreakable love for her." It also troubled him that he felt hurt and angry at her if she cried, didn't respond to him when he wanted her to, or leaned toward her mommy instead of him to soothe and comfort her. He could not tolerate *anything* that felt like abandonment. It is not insignificant that he hates his birthdays and hides them instead of seeking recognition of them—because, as he told me, there are so few people who have really cared about him. With me, it has been no different. He implored me to help him understand himself and his self-destructive behavior, with terror that, otherwise, he would wreck his marriage and make his daughter experience all the pain and have all the problems which he had during his childhood and beyond.

This patient demonstrated repeatedly that he was hungry for closeness, care, and understanding from me, but nevertheless found one excuse after another to cancel sessions; in fact, it seems difficult to keep him from leaving treatment. "The past," as William Faulkner (1951) observed, "is not dead—it's not even past."

CONCLUSION

Not every divorce leads to terrible consequences for the children. There are divorces that take place for very good reasons. They *should* take place. And there are parents who do a very good job of helping their children get through it and deal with its aftermath. There are marriages that are so terrible that the children are done a disservice by their parents *not* ending them. A boy once said to me: "My parents do nothing but fight. They hate each other. They fight all the time. They fight like wild animals. It's horrible. Why don't they get a divorce? My sister and brother and I would be much better off if they *weren't living together!*"

Thinking once again about what that family court judge once said to me about the variety of divorces that came before him, I am inclined to say that divorces are like that little girl in the nursery rhyme who had a little curl in the middle of her forehead. When they are good, they are very, very good—and when they are bad, *they are horrid!* A couple contemplating divorce would do well to think carefully about the effect upon their children of the divorce and of the way in which they handle it—before, during, and afterward. It is incumbent upon those of us who are working with people whose marriage is failing and are heading toward ending it to apprise them of this and help them do it well.

Wallerstein and Blakeslee (2003) have written a book which can be of help to parents titled *What About the Kids? Raising Your Children Before, During, and After Divorce*. Robert Prall, a psychoanalyst who trained and worked in Philadelphia, has written a slim manual (2000), *The Rights of Children in Separation and Divorce: The Essential Handbook for Parents*, that is chock full of sage advice. It is only sixty pages long. On the last page is a sentence that reads: "Remember—you may divorce your spouse, but you can never divorce your children!" (p. 60). I strongly recommend such books to parents who are ending or have ended their marriage, as well as to those in the mental health and legal professions who work with them.

NOTES

1. They have been critiqued for basing their study, at least initially, on data that derived from a self-selected, relatively small sample of subject families who were followed for ten years. This criticism ignores the fact that they subsequently expanded their sample to almost two and a half times the original number, with the additional subjects having been drawn into the study more randomly, and that they followed the whole group, totaling over 160 families, *in depth*, for a total of twenty-five years. There are observational studies of much larger numbers of children of divorce that appear to indicate that divorce is not necessarily hard on children, but they have involved only superficial observation of the children's behavior, *and for only as little as two years*. The conclusions drawn from such short-lived observations of surface behavior impress me as extremely unconvincing. The old adage that you can't tell a book from its cover would appear to apply to such studies.

2. I recently experienced, for example, a mother angrily breaking off the treatment of her child, although she was aware that the child needed it desperately and that the treatment was going well, after I declined to intervene in proceedings she had initiated to block the child's father from access to the child. She did so even after I had explained in detail that doing so would not only enormously jeopardize my ability to help her child clinically but also violate all the precepts of independent, thorough, forensic evaluation of *all* parties concerned which are required in family court legal proceedings.

Chapter Three

The Role of Hostility and Destructive Aggression Between Parents in the Lives of Their Children

Corinne Masur

I will never forget how, at the age of 11, my stepdaughter used to hug her father and me and say "one big happy family." In this way, she poignantly reminded us of her deepest wish—and the deepest wish, I think, of all children—to be a part of one big, happy, ongoing, family.

Perhaps this is something left over from our primitive primate past when survival depended on staying with the group. And perhaps that is where the deep desire for attachment stems from. Just as John Bowlby (1973) and the ethologists taught us, attachment is driven by inborn instincts. Our need to survive, both psychically and physically, comes from a biological imperative, not from instinctual drives. We are social beings, and our well-being depends on emotional closeness and physical proximity to those we love and rely upon, especially early in our lives.

As such, Dr. Silverman has written an important chapter. He makes us look at the potential destructive impact on children of loss through the breakup of the family. In his chapter, Dr. Silverman makes many important points regarding the effect of divorce on children; I will enumerate eight of these:

1. Open hostility between divorcing and divorced parents is disturbing to children—both young and adult—whether they are conscious of it or not.
2. Children may blame themselves for the hostility between their parents and for the eventual separation and divorce, INCLUDING the departure of the parent who leaves the home.
3. If a parent leaves and does not maintain contact with the child, the child's response may be akin to that of a child whose parent has died.
4. Custody arrangements are important and must be made according to the age and stage of development of the child. Young children may be especially adversely affected by multiple changes in location each week.

5. Children may blame the custodial parent for everything and take out the anger he or she has on that parent even though it belongs to the parent who has left.
6. Living in two houses may interfere with children's friendships, with their ability to stay organized, and their feelings of having a TRUE home.
7. Children living with the opposite-sex parent may feel themselves to be the oedipal victor and suffer the consequences of their own guilt regarding this victory.
8. The introduction of stepparents may cause temporary or insoluble loyalty conflicts within the child.

For those of us who care about children, for those of us who treat children, these are crucial points to keep in mind. However, I would like to disrupt this discussion a bit by introducing a few other ideas and an additional perspective. First, I would like to suggest a change in the title of Dr. Silverman's chapter. He calls his chapter, "Divorce Is Not Good for Children and Other Living Things." I would like to alter that to "Hostility Between Parents Is Not Good for Children and Other Living Things."

Why do I want to do this? As Dr. Silverman says, almost 50% of all couples divorce today. With the increasing pressures on the nuclear family and the increased expectations on marital partners to serve all the needs of one another, divorce is not going away. But hostility between parents is even more ubiquitous than divorce. Whether parents stay together, separate, or divorce, hostility may be present. As such, it is very important to think further in order to learn what specifically is harmful to children and what we can do to lessen some of the difficulties of children who experience the divorce of their parents.

Wallerstein and Kelly (1980) are often cited as the experts on divorce given their well-known publications on the destructive impact of divorce on children. When evaluating these findings, it is important to know that their original sample contained only sixty Marin County families and that these families were recruited using newspaper advertisements and flyers offering counselling in exchange for participation. Due at least in part to the quid pro quo of this arrangement, questions have arisen as to whether the population so recruited can be considered random. Moreover, it is possible that such a method of recruitment might attract subjects whose need for mental health services could be greater than those of the general population. According to Ahrons (2009), a certain number of participants were disturbed individuals seeking free treatment. In the appendix of their book, *Surviving the Breakup*, Judith Wallerstein and Joan Kelly state that 50% of their subjects were chronically depressed, sometimes suicidal men and women with chronic problems relating to others and/or with long standing problems in controlling rage or sexual impulses. Of course, it becomes clear that it would have been difficult for Wallerstein and Kelly to sort out the effects of divorce from the effects of having a mentally ill or unstable parent (Ahrons, 2009) on the children involved in the studies. This sampling issue in no way negates all of their findings—but it does suggest caution when looking at the conclusions they make based on these samples. And, of course, their ample clinical material stands on its own.

Hetherington and Kelly (2002), on the other hand, studied 1,400 divorces and 2,500 children. They found, contrary to popular belief, that the consequence of divorce for children are NOT always negative. They state that much of what has been written about divorce has exaggerated the negative effects and ignored some potentially positive effects. In their large longitudinal study, they report that divorce can rescue children from both subtle and overt violence being perpetrated by an angry or disturbed spouse; divorce can result in new freedom for spouses and children to grow psychologically, and divorce can make way for the formation of new, more loving relationships. They state that 75% of children two years after the divorce look identical to their peers from non-divorced families. Moreover, they found that a small percentage of children fell into what they termed "enhanced" functioning where they looked uncommonly resilient, responsible, and focused, not despite the divorce but *because* of it. Similarly, a number of resilience researchers (e.g., Parens, 2008; Southwick, Ozbay, and Mayes, 2008) have proposed that challenges that don't overwhelm the ego may lead to resilience.

Hetherington and Kelly (2002) also found that the two greatest risk factors for children following divorce are the father's absence and the (financial) poverty that may follow divorce. However, they found that if the father was psychologically absent prior to the divorce, his absence had very little negative psychological effect on his children and the children's relationship with him, especially if the children were girls. In fact, in some cases, the effect of the divorce on the relationship between father and child has been found to be positive, as the father may take more responsibility for engaging with the child than previous to the divorce when these functions were seen by the father to be in the domain of the mother.

This brings me to my thesis: One of the most damaging occurrences in the life of a child is severe parental discord and hostility. It is important to note that this is not only present in families where parents divorce. Hostility and destructive aggression are also present in many marriages. And there is danger in a child experiencing destructive aggression between his or her two most beloved objects, whether divorce occurs or not.

When two people fall in love, we know that, due to the transferences they attach to each other, a variety of feelings are stimulated, including hatred, envy, competition, and the wish to destroy the other. Marriage is a dynamic container for the instinctual energies (Piemont, 2009). Depending on the personalities and the intrapsychic and defensive makeup of each partner, not to mention the compatibility of the two partners, the union may be more or less stable and more or less containing. Moreover, the partners may be varyingly willing and/or able to resolve conflict within the relationship and to refrain from the expression of hostile aggressive feelings and impulses within the relationship (Piemont, 2009). With the onslaught of external and/or internal stressors and/or interpersonal conflict, this willingness, even when present, may break down, resulting in open conflict and, in some cases, destructive hostility and violence. As Winnicott (1965) said, healthy development in children depends in part on the parents' capacity to manage their own hostile aggression. Moreover, he stated that each parent (and here I am paraphrasing, as he talked in more gendered terms) requires the other parent to provide support and validation of his or her parenting. This is necessary so that the on-duty parent can be helped to contain the hostile aggression that is inevitably stirred up by the relentless demands of hands-on parenting. When parental hostility ceases to be contained and when parents stop being able to provide nurturance and support for one another as parents, the child is at risk for a variety of reasons.

Failure of the marital relationship to absorb the powerful libidinal energies in either parent leaves the child vulnerable to having these energies inappropriately directed toward him or her. In such instances, the investment in the child of the parents' hostile and libidinal energies may become a serious challenge to the child's sense of well-being and safety and to his ongoing development. The child's ability to tolerate ambivalence—that is, to be able to maintain both positive and negative feelings at the same time for a love object—may be interfered with. When a child witnesses parental hostility expressed within the marital relationship, when he feels it or just intuits it, he may experience a disruption in his normal identificatory processes and wishes. When the identificatory figures model not the tolerance of ambivalence but a turn toward expression of the negative pole in the outpouring of anger, hatred, disgust, or contempt toward the other parent, normal development is heavily burdened and may be disrupted. Not only do children lose their model for containment, but they also experience the unconfined expression of hostile feelings toward a beloved parent. This can be both frightening and terribly painful. Children, who have had the developmentally normal need to contain their own hostility and anger during and following the anal phase, now see that a highly emotionally invested adult, a person who should and generally may have been able to tolerate such feelings without undue outbursts, now cannot contain them. This may interrupt the child's developmental momentum and interfere with the containment of his own hostile aggressive feelings. It is common for children of quarrelling or divorcing parents to feel anger and hatred toward the parents who are displaying hostility toward one another. It is also common for the child to feel anger and hatred for the parent who has left the home, for the custodial parent, OR for the new partner of one parent or the other—and it is common for children in these circumstances to feel anger and hatred toward themselves. The child may also fear anger and hostility in general, his own and that of the parents, affirming his early fear that his and their hostility could become destructive. As such, the child may endeavor to withhold his own anger and hostility, thus becoming passive and constricted. Alternately, he may impulsively discharge hostility in ways that are harmful to himself or to others.

As Dr. Silverman demonstrated, when parents are at odds, the child also feels tremendous loyalty conflicts. Generally children love both of their parents. In fact, the child is aware that he or she is made up of an aggregate of biological and psychological aspects of each parent. All but the youngest children are aware that they are literally part Dad and part Mom. When parents go to war, children can be torn apart; they are unsure who is right and who is wrong, who to side with and who to fight, and they may feel that the parts of themselves that represent each parent are also in conflict or also worthy of hatred or contempt. The loss of the parental unit is unavoidably experienced as a narcissistic loss and as a threat to the sense of self. This may result in a lowering of self-esteem and a perception of the self as damaged, worthless, or unlovable (Lohr et al., 1981).

Over the years, I have seen many children whose parents have been unhappy in their marriages and have argued bitterly and chronically, but who have stayed together. I have also seen many children whose parents have divorced. It is my experience that each situation causes great suffering for the children. For those whose parents do not separate or divorce, there is the ongoing strain trauma of living in a home filled with discord and often outright hostility. Children at all stages of development, but especially those approaching puberty and in adolescence, may feel a terrible burden. Often they feel helpless in the presence of parental fighting. Alternately, they may feel responsible, thinking that they are the cause of the fighting, or they may feel the responsibility to cut back on any stress they may cause either parent for fear of igniting a fight. Often they also feel like it is their job to "fix" one parent or the other or to help their parents to get along. These children sometimes become like little couples' therapists, pointing out to their parents why and how the fights start and feeling frustrated that their parents keep engaging in the same fights over and over again. On the other hand, they may defensively block out the parental fighting, and other parental influences, becoming islands who must precociously function on their own without help from the parents whom they perceive to be out of control. And for those children whose parents do divorce, the change of living situation, the financial changes, and the ongoing hostility that may occur around the division of property, financial matters, custody and other issues can also cause great suffering, strain trauma and, commonly, a retreat into denial and the development of a compensatory reconciliation fantasy. Children in each category suffer.

This brings me to a surprising place: Iceland! Iceland is one of the happiest countries in the world, according to the UN Human Development Index. And Icelanders have one of the highest rates of divorce. They also have one of the highest birth rates among developed nations, and, interestingly for our purposes, Iceland is one of the countries with the lowest number of post-divorce custody battles.

When I was in Iceland a few years ago, I heard an interesting thing: Icelanders do not assume that relationships or marriages are forever. It is common, evidently, for couples to cohabitate or marry for several years, to have children, and then to move on to other relationships. This is expected. But why so few custody battles? After all, human nature being what it is, don't Icelanders feel the same territoriality over their children, the same wishes to control and possess their children as we often do in this country? Evidently not.

In Iceland, according to John Carlin (2008) online in *The Guardian*, there is no stigma attached to divorce. Iceland is not a traditionally Judeo-Christian or Islamic culture. Deities, religious beliefs, and the morality derived from these are not involved in marriage, or separation, or divorce, in Iceland. These are strictly civil matters. According to Roch and Roch (2010), if a relationship does not work, Icelanders simply end it; they do not stay in relationships for fear of religious reprisal. Anecdotal evidence suggests that there is less acrimony between spouses following separation and children are seldom used as pawns.

Some writers suggest that this is the legacy of the Viking past in Iceland when husbands traveled the seas for years and had to accept whatever progeny they found at home on their return, regardless of the patrimony. Furthermore, Icelandic law dictates that custody decisions are made in the best interests of the child at all times. "Every child in Iceland has the right to spend time with his or her non-custodial parent and it is the responsibility of both parents to see that equitable visitation schedules are established and maintained. If the parents fail to do so, the courts will set up a visitation schedule to assure this access" (Emery, 2013, p. 92).

Carlin (2008) observed in *The Guardian*, "It is common for women to have children with more than one man—but all are family together." The incentives for staying together for the sake of the children, according to one Icelander cited in the article, do not exist because it is assumed that everyone will rally round the children if parents separate and the parents will have a civilized relationship based on a universally automatic understanding that custody of the children will be shared. In a radio documentary on the topic, an Icelandic attorney said, "We prioritize the children, not the parents; parents put the children in the foreground and set their own differences aside" (Hlunur Jonsson from the Icelandic Airways Documentary, 2015).

So, if we look at the Icelandic experience, we can see that it is not necessarily divorce or separation itself that causes the hostile destructive conflicts that injure children and disrupt families. Families can, in fact, continue to care for children in a civilized manner post-divorce. If we use the Icelandic example, we can hypothesize that cultural and religious factors affect assumptions about marriage and relationships in general. If it is stigmatizing to divorce, if it is seen as a failure in the culture or within the individual's family or religious tradition, it can be inferred that couples feel pressure to stay together longer, to withstand more discord, to remain together indefinitely, or to wait until conditions are intolerable to take the steps toward separation and divorce.

Again, it is my premise that what is most damaging to children is just this: the escalation of hostility and the display of such feeling between two beloved objects. And this is backed by the literature. In a review of recent studies, researchers consistently found that high levels of parental conflict during and after divorce are associated with poorer adjustment in the children (Arkowitz and Lilienfeld, 2012).

This hostility then generates further difficulty post-separation or divorce in the former spouses' ability to work together as parents. An overabundance of negative feeling can persevere and can pollute the parenting role. Moreover, the presence of ongoing hostility may be the cause of a loss of involvement or a diminution of involvement by the noncustodial parent. Accordingly, as Hetherington and Kelly (2002) found, quite damaging to children is the noncustodial fathers' difficulty in functioning as fathers. It turns out that in our society many men, regardless of the educational level, just don't know how to relate to their children in the fathering role.

So how do we help children best? How do we ameliorate the effects in our culture of parental hostility, separation, and divorce? What do we learn from the research and from the Icelanders? Obviously, we need to bring into our culture the idea, the value, that children are everyone's responsibility. It is often said that children are the future, but if this is the case, we don't seem to care sufficiently about the future in the United States; we don't invest sufficiently in the future in this particular sense. We need to provide the popular will and the monetary support needed for universal day care, universal pre-kindergarten, good schools, and after-school programs for working parents (whether divorced or not) and programs to help all parents and especially single parents, fathers in particular, to learn how to be good parents and to enjoy and derive gratification from their relationships with their children.

Moreover, we need to rethink our patients' roles as partners and as parents, and our own. Perhaps it is time to divorce ourselves from the old dictates of religion and accept, as have the Icelanders, the inevitability that some relationships will last and some will not, and that, for the good of our children, one of most important and enduring roles for many of us are not husband or wife but parents.

And, most important, we need to continue to think about the effect of anger, hostility, hatred, and contempt in couples on their children. I have thought for a long while that anger and hostility are the least well-tolerated emotions in our society. In relationships, there is always ambivalence, but when the relationship is ongoing, the ambivalence may be held, the negative side tolerated and contained. At times of conflict in the parental relationship, the ambivalence can become uncontainable; the negative side is expressed, while the positive side is dimnished or kept silent. When children are exposed to unconfined negative affects expressed by one parent toward the other, they may be confused and frightened; they may feel threatened both physically and psychically. If parents are not able to process their own hostility within themselves or with each other, they may not be able to help their children to process, understand, and metabolize these feelings. In such cases, children are at great risk.

As stated, children exposed to the hostility and hatred of one parent for another are torn, their loyalties are tested, their own ability to tolerate negative feelings is stretched and they are overwhelmed with pain and suffering—that of their mother, that of their father, and their own. In conclusion, divorce can be damaging for children, but whether parents divorce or whether they stay together, it is the hostility and hatred, the dissolution of the containment of these feelings, and the maintenance of healthy ambivalence toward the partner that is the most destructive factor for the children involved. Cooperative co-parenting, in both married and divorced families, is a major protective factor for all developing children.

Chapter Four

Some Countertransference Challenges in Working with Divorcing Adults

Joshua Ehrlich

Divorce, at its core, usually involves a wrenching experience of loss. A divorcing person loses his or her spouse, extended family connections, and an established way of life. Even if a marriage has been difficult and unfulfilling, a divorcing person loses hope for a stable, loving marriage to his or her spouse. Much (but not all) of the literature on divorce describes loss in simple terms. Psychoanalytic thinkers appreciate that the loss of a relationship is multidimensional and depends on the meanings of the loss for a particular person. While there is a great deal of psychoanalytic writing on loss by death, there is surprisingly little on the losses of divorce.

The loss of a marriage is inevitably the repetition of earlier losses. When those losses have been traumatic, divorce can be traumatic, too. For instance, when a person has suffered early narcissistic trauma and the marital partner serves important self-object functions, the loss of the marriage, especially if one is left, can represent further narcissistic traumatization (Ehrlich, 2014). The possible meanings of divorce are infinite. When children are involved, divorce has even more complicated and troubling ramifications for adults, as we all are aware.

As therapists/analysts, we work with divorce in any number of contexts. Sometimes, people come to us because they feel paralyzed: Should they divorce or not? We also see adults in the throes of divorce. A person might have learned, for instance, that a spouse is having an affair and comes to us overwhelmed with grief and shock. Still others seek help a few years post-divorce because they are unable to get back on their feet emotionally for reasons they cannot comprehend. Some of us see children and adolescents bereft and outraged by their parents' decision to end their marriage and, from the child's point of view, to tear their families apart.

While all of us in clinical practice deal with divorce, we probably do not see divorce as a specialized area that requires some careful scrutiny, unless, perhaps, we get caught up in some clinical or ethical bind, or, as I do, conduct child custody evaluations and mediation. After all, in working with divorce, we are dealing with what we might call bread-and-butter clinical issues: loss, anger, regret, difficulties with intimacy, abandonment, and so on. I am going to suggest here, though, that it is worth stepping back and considering some of the challenges that arise in working with adults who are contemplating or are in the midst of divorce or are struggling to manage post-divorce. More specifically, I am going to illustrate some countertransference challenges that are common in working with divorce and, if ignored or misunderstood and acted out, can lead to clinical interventions that are unhelpful, even destructive. Sometimes, failure to take heed of these challenges leads to egregious ethical lapses, which I will discuss briefly as well.

DEFENSES AGAINST LOSS

I am going to use clinical vignettes to illustrate the kinds of issues I want to bring to your attention. Before doing so, I want to briefly examine a topic that all of us know a great deal about but, in the context of divorce, can lose track of: defenses. In the face of the many losses in divorce, adults put defenses into place to manage overwhelming feelings. Some engage in serial sexual relationships in the hope that, in brief exciting encounters, they can escape sorrow. Perhaps, too, in brief affairs, they can regain some of the self-object functions they have lost in the spouse (being admired for being attractive, for instance). Others immerse themselves in substance use or other compulsive behaviors. Many people, in the face of loss, become angry. They denigrate the spouse, or regress into acrimonious interactions over custody or property, or who did what to whom in an effort to keep feelings of sadness, guilt, and shame at abeyance.

In many instances, it can be easy for people, even therapists, to lose track of the sorrow catalyzed by divorce. Bitter arguments, dramatic court battles or the sudden immersion in a passionate love affair can leave the impression that the losses were not so great. In contrast to loss by death, where we intuitively grasp the enormity of the loss and participate in rituals, such as *shiva*, to help us process it (Slochower, 1993), the losses of divorce often are more inchoate and buried, and we lack such rituals (Betz and Thorngren, 2006).

MOURNING

I would suggest that, in the years following a separation and divorce, the central psychological task for adults is mourning. Kogan (2007), in her book,

The Struggle Against Mourning, offers what I find to be a helpful definition. Mourning is

> the conglomerate of favorable processes that develop in the face of loss. It includes acceptance of reality and readaptation to it. Mourning means acceptance of one's perpetual vulnerability to loss and betrayal, as well as to one's own limitations and to the finality of life. (p. 1)

We can think of mourning in response to divorce as involving movement, usually gradual and painstaking, from denial or outrage or defensive acting out to some sense of resolution about the end of the marriage, including a capacity to reflect earnestly on one's own limitations and the limitations of the ex-spouse. It allows one to move on energetically with one's life, including, if one chooses, engaging fully in new romantic relationships. Hetherington and Kelly (2002), in their longitudinal study of divorce, found that over the course of three to four years, most people rewrite what the authors call their "divorce scripts," moving from visions of being victimized to being coconspirators in the demise of the marriage. We might think of the rewriting of a "divorce script" as emblematic of a constructive mourning process.

In order to mourn, a person needs to be able, at least some of the time, to be aware of and bear the underlying feelings of sorrow and grief and regret that come with the end of an important relationship. That is no mean feat. People implement defenses because they have run into affect states they find intolerable. It is often much easier to fight than to weep. In working with adults around divorce, we might think of ourselves as facilitators of mourning, helping our patients develop a greater tolerance for the feelings they seek to disavow.

CHALLENGES FOR THERAPISTS OF
DEALING WITH MOURNING PATIENTS

Here, we move into the topic of countertransference. It is often more comfortable, less painful, for therapists to align with their patients' defenses than to have to bear the difficult feelings that emerge when we steadily address defensive shifts away from underlying affects. However, if we fall into that trap, we cannot help our patients mourn.

Schlesinger (2001) addressed challenges in analyzing patients who are mourning. He described the analyst's wish to spare our loved ones, including our patients and ourselves,

> pain of any kind, and in particular, prolonged pain, and we may feel impelled to alleviate *our* distress by intervening to ameliorate their suffering. It takes great

discipline to allow a patient ... to experience the process of grieving and mourning fully and to appreciate, and help them appreciate, the importance of doing so. (p. 124, emphasis added)

Schlesinger argues that it is always hard for therapists to deal with the effects associated with mourning. I would add here that facilitating mourning around divorce presents additional challenges because therapists must withstand powerful pulls that can easily derail them from the facilitating role they need to assume.

Clinical vignette: 1

Denying loss through disavowing love

Mr. A. is a successful professional man in his 40s in the process of a divorce. He has two teenage daughters and calls asking for help because, he says, he is concerned about one of his daughters, who is acting out. In the initial consultation, Mr. A. talks briefly about his daughter but then shifts to a discussion of his twenty-year marriage and his bitterness at what he sees as his wife's constant unhappiness, her criticisms of him, and her failure to create a stable work life. Mr. A. reveals that he has been having an affair with a colleague. He contrasts this woman's passion and warmth to his wife, whom he describes as distant and devoid of sexual passion. He paints a picture of a marriage that has lacked intimacy for years. He expresses anxiety that he and his wife are on the verge of a nasty struggle in court around distribution of their property.

At the beginning of the twice-weekly therapy, I found myself taken in by Mr. A.'s description of his wife, who came across as brittle, unpleasant, and retaliatory. I thought that Mr. A. was fortunate to be escaping such a marriage and found his description of his new love affair compelling. I became aware of an image developing in my mind of his wife: a small, shrewish woman whose coldness would drive any man into the arms of another woman. Over the course of a few months, though, I gradually became aware that Mr. A.'s narrative seemed incomplete: His wife was so awful; his new lover was so terrific. And Mr. A., despite his ostensible delight at the new relationship, often seemed downcast and subdued. I began to think I had gotten caught up in his defensive need to turn a complex, even tragic situation—a twenty-year marriage ending with an affair—into a purely positive one. Though I felt Mr. A.'s sadness about the divorce, I become aware that he never talked about it.

A few months into the therapy, I said to Mr. A.: "I appreciate that your marriage came to feel awful to you and you are pleased to be getting a divorce. At the same time, I find it a bit hard to believe that the marriage was as awful as you describe. Can you tell me about some close times with your wife?" Mr. A. sat quietly for a few minutes, pondered and then began to cry. He sat weeping for several minutes. When he was able to talk, he expressed shock that he was so sad because he had no idea he felt that way. He told me that, as he sat there crying, he was thinking of the first several years of the marriage when he and his wife were close and passionate and full of dreams about the future. While they had drifted far apart over the last several years, he once had loved her dearly.

In the months that followed, Mr. A. began to mourn the end of his marriage in earnest. He cried in recalling family vacations with their daughters. He allowed himself, with sorrow, to remember sexual intimacy with his wife. In reflecting briefly on this clinical situation, we can say that Mr. A., as he initiated a divorce process, was unable to tolerate his sorrow about the loss of a woman who, at one point, had been dear to him. He erected defenses against feeling that loss by blocking out awareness of loving feelings. For a time, he was able to draw me into an alliance with his defences—reflected in the almost entirely negative image of his wife that I developed in my mind. When I was able to tune myself more fully into Mr. A.'s sorrow, I was able to begin to help him mourn the end of his marriage. But I had to relinquish my own defensive needs to see his wife in negative terms and bear his grief.

In a 1990 paper, "Transference and Countertransference in Clinical Interventions with Divorcing Families," Judith Wallerstein, the most prominent writer on divorce (who, by the way, incorporated a psychodynamic perspective), suggested that the "reversal of love into hate" is frightening for all of us. She asks: "Who among us is immune to the mundane conflicts of marriage, the difficulties in sustaining intimacy, the minor and major lapses in all marriages that inevitably threaten [their] continuity?" (p. 338). She suggests that therapists, out of anxiety, are vulnerable to distancing themselves from their patients or, conversely, overidentifying with them. Just as divorce has idiosyncratic meanings for the spouses involved, it has such meanings for therapists, too. A few analysts (Shane, 2002; Basecu, 2009) have described the often wrenching experience of working therapeutically with divorce while they themselves were divorcing. Therapists who had to suffer through their parents' divorce in childhood inevitably bring those experiences to the therapeutic interaction.

With Mr. A., for my own personal reasons, it was easier for me initially to take some pleasure in his harsh, dismissive portrait of his wife than to open myself up to the tragedy in the situation; however, that reverberated in my own psyche. I would add a piece to this picture that I will address in more detail below when I talk about the high-conflict divorce: Mr. A., unconsciously, pressured me to buttress his defensive distancing from his loving feelings (and the sorrow that attached to them).

Clinical vignette: 2

Denying loss through denying hard realities

While some people like Mr. A. defend against the losses of divorce by exaggerating the spouse's liabilities and downplaying his or her strengths, others do essentially the opposite: They attempt to block out awareness of the spouse's negative features through denial and idealization in order to fend off awareness of underlying disappointment about the limitations of the spouse and the potential demise of the marriage. Such situations create different sorts of pressures on therapists.

Ms. B., a sharp, tough-minded accountant, began an analysis as she struggled to sort out what to do about her strained marriage. She had grown up with a father with bipolar disorder who, when he was not taking medication, raged against family members and, at times, was violent. She described how, as a girl, she and other family members tended to deny the severity of her father's mental illness, by describing him, alternately, as "energetic" and "hyper." In her treatment, she gradually came to see how overwhelmed she had felt by her father's behaviors and how little help she had gotten from her mother in dealing with them.

In the early stages of her analysis, Ms. B. alternated between a focus on her husband's positive features—his intelligence, business successes, lively personality—and her sinking feeling she had been taken in by him. She had found credit card receipts that indicated he was spending up to $1,000/month on strip clubs and she also found evidence of cocaine use. At first, she denied what she saw and assumed she was exaggerating her concerns. As evidence accrued, though, she mustered the courage to confront her husband who told her: Yes, he went to strip clubs but did so for business purposes. He denied substance use and told Ms. B. she was overreacting and needed to trust him. Shortly after that conversation, Ms. B. received an alarming communication from her husband's business partner that their business was floundering and was on the brink of bankruptcy.

During the early months of the analysis, I wondered if Ms. B. were downplaying her husband's liabilities. I admired Ms. B., who had worked with great diligence and competence to create a viable adult life after her difficult childhood. I wondered whether this intelligent woman could be so recklessly blind to reality. In identification with her, though, I became fuzzy in my thinking at times, wondering if I, too, was exaggerating the severity of the problem and then, alternately, recognizing just how bad things had become. In retrospect, I think that I also became a participant in the reenactment of a family drama: I was the mother who, for her own defensive needs, was unable to help her daughter process harsh reality.

As time passed and the data became more compelling, I came to understand that Ms. B. was, indeed, defensively shutting out awareness of her husband's disturbed behaviors in a desperate effort to avoid facing the loss of the longed-for and idealized marital partner. Having grown up with a troubled father, she could not bear to recognize that her husband—the wished-for antidote to her tumultuous childhood family life—was troubled himself. I realized that I was feeling upset by the reality of her husband's disturbance and its implications for her life. I felt Ms. B. had suffered enough and deserved a stable, loving marriage.

As I recognized my defensive denial, I began to confront Ms. B. with hers. When she proposed that she was being hysterical by making such a big deal, I suggested that she preferred seeing herself as hysterical to recognizing she was observing something disturbing. Here, I was addressing Ms. B.'s omnipotent defense: the problem was her hysteria, not that she was powerless in the face of his acting-out behaviors. When Ms. B. denied clear signs of cocaine abuse, I suggested she would rather relinquish the use of her excellent mind than use it to see something that was so upsetting. I compared her precision and acumen at work to her vagueness and uncertainty in relation to her husband.

Over the course of several months, Ms. B. began to acknowledge more fully that her husband was out of control and her marriage was untenable. She confronted her utter devastation at her betrayal by a man whom she needed. Finally, being able to see clearly the stark reality that lay before her and continuing to mourn, Ms. B. filed for divorce.

TOLERATING AMBIVALENCE

In the months surrounding a marital separation when feelings about loss are most raw, it can be almost impossible for a person to stay attuned to both the negative and positive features of a marital relationship. A person's need to hold tightly to the negative features, as Mr. A. did, blocks out awareness of sorrow at saying goodbye but impedes the necessary awareness that something good has been lost. Conversely, idealizing the spouse, as Ms. B. did, obstructs the awareness of realistic disappointment that is necessary for mourning. While such defensive stances may be adaptive initially, over time, the person's ability to tolerate ambivalence by integrating the negative and positive features of the relationship—or, put differently, the loving and hating elements—is crucial to mourning. This is a point made by Nehami Baum (2004, 2006, 2006a), a psychoanalytic social worker in Israel, who wrote a compelling series of papers on mourning divorce, incorporating a Kleinian perspective.

In this context, we can suggest that therapists' role is to facilitate the tolerance of ambivalence by helping divorcing adults bring into awareness elements of the relationship they have defensively split off so they can reframe the marriage in more complex terms. In order to fulfil that task, therapists have to find ways to appreciate marital relationships in all of their dimensions. We can conceptualize a common countertransference acting out in terms of therapists allying themselves with one side of their patients' ambivalence and thus failing to facilitate its resolution or, even more problematically, contributing to a rigidifying of defenses. We see this phenomenon most glaringly and frequently in the context of the high-conflict divorce.

THE HIGH-CONFLICT DIVORCE AND
THE CLINICAL/ETHICAL LAPSES THAT
CAN OCCUR IN SUCH SITUATIONS

While only 15% of parents report "intense" conflict over divorce, highly conflicted divorces take up about 90% of family courts' attention (Coates and Fieldstone, 2008). The concept of high-conflict divorce has been somewhat ambiguous in the literature. Coates and Fieldstone (2008) offer a useful definition:

> These parents engage in conflict that is ongoing and unresolved and that intensifies after the divorce or separation rather than diminishing. [The parties] litigate and re-litigate over minor and inconsequential issues generated by their own need to control or punish each other, often obstructing access to the children. (p. 9)

Though high-conflict divorces are more volatile and inflammatory than more ordinary divorces, their dynamics are essentially the same—two people struggling emotionally to disengage from a (presumably) close relationship and employing defenses to deal with painful affects. And, though exhausting and potentially treacherous to work with, high-conflict divorces are especially instructive because they expose clinicians in highly crystallized, vivid ways to interpersonal forces they will encounter in all divorces.

I use the language "potentially treacherous" because clinicians working with the high-conflict divorce are extremely vulnerable to committing clinical blunders and ethical transgressions unless they understand well the forces they are dealing with. Sometimes, clinicians will have worked for years with a high-conflict divorce without ever understanding how little they comprehended of the family situation and how they contributed to its deterioration. Other times, the situation will explode—a licensing complaint, for instance—and they will realize they are caught in a storm they were unaware was engulfing them. Let me offer two brief clinical vignettes to illustrate what I am describing.

Clinical vignette: 3

Mr. C., seeking an ally in his custody battle over his 11-year-old son, arranges a consultation with a local psychiatrist. An articulate, forceful man, Mr. C. explains in compelling detail how his wife displays the symptoms of a severe borderline personality disorder and is enmeshed dangerously with their son. He also paints a picture of himself as an almost flawless parent who has devoted himself selflessly to his son's care. The psychiatrist, alarmed by Mr. C.'s description and eager to help this impassioned father, writes a letter to the court supporting Mr. C.'s contention that he should have full custody.

The psychiatrist committed an ethical lapse by making recommendations about custody without conducting a full evaluation (which would involve both parents, the child(ren), and an order of the court). She also reinforced Mr. C.'s retaliatory stance toward his wife. When confronted about her role, the psychiatrist became defensive, insisting she had ample data to make the assessment she did and was ethically obligated to protect the child from his mother. She was so convinced by Mr. C.'s account that she could not begin to consider that the situation was more complicated than Mr. C. had indicated.

This sort of miscue plays itself out in individual therapy, too, when therapists get caught up in their patients' simplistic accounts of their marriages and divorces and blindly align with them without considering that they, for defensive reasons, are distorting the reality of what is going on.

Clinical vignette: 4

Ms. W., a tough-minded mediator, was progressing in her work with Mr. D. and Ms. D., a divorced couple who had been battling angrily for months around property and their children's care. She was pleased when she finally was able to get the parents to agree to Mr. D.'s suggestion of a psychiatric evaluation for their adolescent son, who was depressed and possibly suicidal. But Ms. W. was stunned when the mother stormed into the next mediation session and asserted that she was no longer willing to support a psychiatric evaluation. She elaborated that she had spoken to her own therapist, who had told her she was being bullied by her ex-husband and urged her to put her foot down. The mediator was perplexed that Ms. D.'s therapist had so profoundly misunderstood the circumstances because she had worked hard to ensure Ms. D.'s voice was heard during the mediation and believed that Mr. D.'s request for the psychiatric consultation was appropriate to the circumstances, not a maneuver to gain some sort of power. She wondered why, if this psychologist were so concerned, he had not gotten a consent from his patient to speak with her so that he could better understand the mediator's view of the family situation. Ms. D.'s therapist likely viewed himself as a passionate advocate on behalf of his vulnerable patient and apparently never considered that Ms. D. was using him as a weapon in the battle with her ex-husband. Ms. D.'s therapist, by exacerbating Ms. D.'s righteous outrage at her ex-husband, contributed to an unfortunate escalation of tension between the parents and failed to help his patient come to terms with the end of her marriage.

COMMON DEFENSES IN THE HIGH-CONFLICT DIVORCE

Understanding the defenses people employ when they lock into conflict provides a framework for understanding the powerful pressures on therapists that lead to the sorts of clinical lapses noted above. Most of the people we work with around divorce use what George Vaillant (1977), in *Adaptation to Life*, calls neurotic and mature defenses. Among neurotic defenses, Vaillant includes intellectualization, displacement, and repression; he includes sublimation and humor among mature defenses. Critical for our discussion of mourning, we can observe that people who use neurotic and mature defenses tend to maintain enough access to painful underlying affects that, over time, especially with help, they can engage in a constructive mourning process. We can see how Mr. A.'s and Ms. B.'s defenses, though powerful, were workable and, gradually, they were able to integrate the sorrow stimulated by the end of their marriages. Not surprisingly, many people who lock into bitter, ongoing acrimony suffered early losses or massive narcissistic traumas. According to Jan Johnston, the foremost writer and researcher on the high-conflict divorce (who also integrates psychodynamic ideas into her writing), about two thirds of people in high-conflict divorces have Axis II diagnoses, including para-noid, borderline and schizoid personality disorders. For many of these people, the losses and narcissistic injuries inherent in divorce are, essentially, more than they can manage psychically. Old losses surface, overwhelming them. If they have been left, the narcissistic mortification is more than they can bear. They implement what Vaillant (1977) would characterize as psychotic and immature defenses (e.g., splitting, distortion, delusional projection), which rigidly and ferociously block access to underlying feelings of grief, shame, and guilt.

Such defenses are adaptive in a sense, in that, much of the time, they suc-cessfully fend off awareness of painful affects. But, of course, they come at a price. They tend to contribute to interpersonal conflict and interfere with empathy, moral functioning, and self-reflectiveness. And, because they do not allow the access to affects that is essential to mourning, they impede it, contributing to individuals staying locked into the same feuds, sometimes for many years.

A person like Mr. C., who roped the psychiatrist into writing a letter to the court, relies on the defense of splitting, whereby negative self-attributes such as hostility and envy are attributed to another person. In resorting to splitting, Mr. C. frees himself of ideas of badness and burdensome responsibility for negative behaviors by making his wife the repository for those experiences of himself. By disowning responsibility for his role in the demise of the marriage, Mr. C. protects his fragile self-esteem. By viewing his wife as dis-turbed, he can also invalidate reasons for having loved her (how could he love someone so awful?), thus assuring himself that there was no reason to feel sad about losing her. Unfortunately, Mr. C.'s rigid defensive stance renders impossible the central tasks of mourning: that is, being aware of his love and his sadness about loss, reflecting on his own role in the divorce.

SOME COUNTERTRANSFERENCE CHALLENGES IN WORKING WITH THE HIGH-CONFLICT DIVORCE

Working with the high-conflict divorce can have a nightmarish quality. Because these patients are unable (or barely able) to mourn, we can feel as if we were going through Bill Murray's experience in the 1993 movie, *Groundhog Day*—waking up and finding that every day is exactly the same. It can also be troubling because parents in high-conflict divorces tend to do awful things to their children—like maligning their other parent or interfering with the parent's access to the child—and feel entirely justified in doing so. Maintaining empathy for a parent in such a situation can be extremely difficult.

We can find ourselves lashing out critically at patients who are least able to tolerate it narcissistically. Working with people in acrimonious divorces is most treacherous when therapists are insufficiently aware of the force field that surrounds them. Of particular importance is that people like Mr. C. urgently need others to fortify their fragile defenses and are likely to pull therapists into that role. Johnston and Campbell (1988), in their nuanced, multilayered explication of the high-conflict divorce, describe what they term "tribal warfare," a process in which friends, families, attorneys, and even mental health professionals line up on one side or another of ugly disputes over custody. The feuding parties' positions are so rigidly black and white that it is almost impossible to carve out some kind of middle space. One is *for* them or *against* them.

It is not uncommon for the attorneys and therapists of warring parents to engage in nasty disputes themselves, each convinced that his or her patient/client is being victimized by the spouse (or ex-spouse) and enraged the other professional fails to understand the "true story." Even after almost 30 years of working with high-conflict divorces, I continue to be impressed by family law attorneys who are fully convinced that every aggrieved party they represent is the true victim and the other parent the perpetrator of myriad transgressions. I want to ask them: "What are the odds that every parent you have represented in a high-conflict divorce is completely unblemished and the spouse the victimizer?"

In contrast to most divorcing people, who genuinely seek help from therapists with their psychic pain, people like Mr. C. seek confirmation of their views of the bad character of the spouse and vindication of their own behaviors and character. Such individuals indicate that their views regarding the ex-spouse are obvious and that anybody with any sense—much less a therapist with presumed diagnostic acumen—will see the situation as they do. Therapists discern immediately, though not always consciously, that these parents are under enormous internal pressure, desperately erecting barriers against a flood of inner feelings, like a person frantically stacking sand bags to protect a home from onrushing water.

We, as therapists, in order to form alliances with their patients, work hard to find ways to experience them as likeable, even when their behaviors are aversive. We want to help and want people to appreciate our skills, including our capacities for empathy. We become aware we will face our patient's disdain, if not outright rage, if we do not accept that person's views of the divorce, including the harsh assessment of the spouse. We will be labeled insensitive or hurtful—one more on a list of unkind people in that person's life. The pressures that feuding individuals place on therapists dovetail with therapists' natural tendencies to side with their patients' perspectives. This contributes to the chances that therapists will align themselves with their patients' defensively driven views of a family situation, rather than bearing the acute discomfort of calling those views into question (Ehrlich, 2014).

SOME KEYS TO AVOIDING MISSTEPS IN WORKING WITH THE HIGH-CONFLICT DIVORCE

Therapists who lack experience with the high-conflict divorce are especially vulnerable to patients' accusations of insensitivity and to believing they actually were unkind or unempathic, as opposed to recognizing that it is almost impossible to question the views of a person absorbed in chronic feuding without provoking a fierce backlash. It can be very helpful when therapists recognize as early as possible that they are working with a high-conflict divorce, so they can contextualize clinical interactions accurately. Protracted litigation usually indicates a high-conflict divorce. In addition, if a parent presents a unidimensional account with a highly critical description of the spouse (or ex-spouse), the clinician should take heed. Baris et al. (2001) offer a Conflict Assessment Scale that can help clinicians identify a high-conflict divorce early. It categorizes conflict along a spectrum from minimal to severe and provides specific criteria for assessment. Chethik et al. (1984) suggest that clinicians working with divorced parents must clarify their patients' level of narcissistic disturbance before they can know how to pitch interventions. They differentiate among transitory narcissistic stress, narcissistic regression, and severe narcissistic vulnerability (exacerbated by the divorce). It is also important for therapists to be able to bear ambiguity while they try to figure out what exactly is going on with their patients, as in the following example.

Clinical vignette: 5

Ms. E., two years after a nasty divorce, sought help dealing with what she described vaguely as her ex-husband's persistent antagonism. Her therapist, experienced with high-conflict divorces, was wary. He wanted to help Ms. E. but did not want to exacerbate a chronically tense family situation by simply agreeing with her in what he thought might be a defensive need to exaggerate her ex-husband's liabilities. He listened carefully and waited to sort the situation out. Eventually, Ms. E. brought in emails from her ex-husband in which he described her as a "bitch" and a "whore." While Ms. E. found these upsetting, she wondered if she were exaggerating her ex-husband's disturbance. She related, almost in passing, that her ex-husband had followed her a few times when she went on dates. She was troubled by this behavior, but, again, wondered if she were "overreacting." It became clear to the therapist that Ms. E.'s primary problem was not a defensive need to exaggerate her ex-husband's psychopathology, as many high-conflict parents do, but the opposite: She defensively downplayed the depth of his disturbance because she found it so scary and unsettling.

If therapists choose to work with individuals in the midst of high-conflict divorces, they can use these patients' defenses as guideposts to assess if they are warding off painful feelings associated with loss by exaggerating the ex-spouse's difficult qualities or, alternatively, if they, like Ms. E., are defensively downplaying the ex-spouse's psychological problems because of difficulties bearing that harsh reality.

Traumatic separations between spouses (involving violence, for instance, or sudden departures) can consolidate into patterns of recrimination and retribution, so early intervention is essential when these occur (Johnston, Roseby, and Kuehnle, 2009). When a therapist working individually with a parent sees a serious escalation in tensions, referral to a professional who can intervene within the structure of a court order (a mediator, arbitrator, parenting coordinator) is in order. If we conceptualize feuding as a way to fend off underlying sorrow, shame, and guilt, then we can frame any intervention that seeks to diminish feuding—for example, collaborative divorce—as potentially facilitating a mourning process for the parties involved. It behooves therapists to know about alternative modes of dispute resolution so that, potentially, they can steer their patients in the most helpful direction.

Johnston et al. (2009) argue that working with people involved in high-conflict divorces without an overarching structure and purpose is a "prescription for disaster" (p. 258). Accordingly, they recommend that all interventions take place within the structure of a court order that coordinates the activities of the clinicians involved. For therapists who specialize in work with high-conflict divorce and are accustomed to collaborating within the structure of a court order, such an arrangement might feel comfortable. For many others, though, especially those who primarily conduct individual therapy, such a process runs contrary to their usual practice. It may not occur to them, caught up as they are in their individual work, that simply agreeing with their patients' perceptions of the marriage and divorce could exacerbate a deteriorating family situation. In stepping into a high-conflict divorce, though, all of us have clinical and ethical obligations to consider the impact of our interventions on the family as a whole.

Chapter Five

Transference and Countertransference in the Divorce Process

A Psycho-legal Challenge for Lawyers and Judges

Stephen J. Anderer

This contribution represents an intellectual homecoming for me, back to the psychodynamic foundation of my graduate training in clinical psychology. Since completing my predoctoral internship in clinical psychology twenty-three years ago, I have been working as a lawyer. The majority of my legal work has been with men and women who are in the process of getting divorced from their spouses, helping them to resolve the variety of issues that arise during that process, including financial and child custody issues. My participation in the 47th Annual Margaret S. Mahler Symposium on Child Development, and specifically the request that I comment on Dr. Joshua Ehrlich's chapter, "Some Countertransference Challenges in Working with Divorcing Adults," caused me to think more deeply about the psychodynamic aspects of the interactions that I have been observing in my family law practice over these years.

THE INTENSITY OF EMOTION
AND RELATIONSHIPS IN DIVORCE

I agree with Dr. Ehrlich that divorce is a specialized area that requires careful scrutiny. For one, during divorce, people frequently reach their emotional extremes—whether that extreme is debilitating anxiety, depression to the point of suicidality, or anger to the point of homicidality. If a lawyer works as a divorce lawyer for any length of time, the odds are high that someone he or she works with, or an opposing party, will commit suicide. When newspapers (or in this day and age, newsfeeds) report that someone fired shots at a courthouse or killed a spouse, almost inevitably, the second line of the story is that he (or less likely she) was involved in a difficult divorce or child custody litigation.

A quick story highlights the intensity of the emotions in divorce. I had the misfortune to be involved in what was at one time called the "Main Line's messiest divorce" (the "Main Line" being the name given to certain wealthy suburbs of Philadelphia). In that case, the husband set the United States record for the longest incarceration for civil contempt—that is, for not following a judge's order. He spent fourteen years in jail rather than follow the judge's order to turn over money.

But that is not the international record. The international record was set in Israel, where, in order for the wife to get a divorce, the husband needed to give the wife a "get"—essentially, the husband had to consent to the divorce. In that case, when the husband would not give his wife a "get," he was ordered to jail. He spent thirty-two years in jail and died in jail rather than giving his wife a divorce. The money was not an issue in that case, but the husband was able to prevent his wife from remarrying.

A second reason why divorce is a psychodynamically rich area that deserves special scrutiny is because of the multiple intense relationships. Dr. Ehrlich's chapter discusses the dynamics of the spousal relationships and the therapist–patient relationships during divorce. However, in many instances in his chapter, you could substitute the word lawyer for therapist, because the dynamic between the individual and his or her lawyer is similar to the dynamic between the individual and his or her therapist. There are intense transference and countertransference phenomena in the lawyer–client relationship, and Dr. Ehrlich touches on some of them.

There are other intense relationships in the divorce context that are also worth exploring—the relationship of a divorcing spouse with the opposing lawyer, for example. I have found it fascinating to see the thoughts and feelings that my clients direct toward the other lawyer or that the opposing party may direct toward me. The other lawyer—or I—may be seen by the opposing party as evil personified. Meanwhile, lawyers may themselves have very intense reactions to opposing parties, and those reactions may influence the behaviors of the lawyers.

In addition, the relationships that parties have with other actors within the court system can become grist for the therapeutic mill. Very intense transference and countertransference reactions can occur between parties and judges. A party may invest a judge with many different characteristics, both positive and negative, and a judge may respond to a party in a manner that is influenced not simply by the objective response to facts, but by the judge's own psychodynamic makeup.

THERAPEUTIC JURISPRUDENCE

"Therapeutic jurisprudence" is a school of inquiry that looks at the psychological sequelae of legal rules and procedures and how we might change those rules and procedures to increase the positive psychological sequelae and decrease the negative (Stolle, Wexler, and Winick, 2000). In other words, how do we adjust what is done in the legal system to make it less destructive, and perhaps, even therapeutic? One way to start is to educate not just therapists about transference and countertransference phenomena in the divorce context but also lawyers and judges.

It is easy for lawyers to get drawn in by their clients' narratives. Some lawyers who see their roles only as "advocates" will take their clients' perspective at face value and run with it or even exaggerate it. It may be worthwhile to teach more lawyers about their roles as "counselors" whose thoughtful examination of their clients' perspectives can provide a great service to their clients. Dr. Ehrlich's chapter would be a good start toward helping lawyers understand the psyche of their clients who, like Mr. A., go to an extreme in denigrating a spouse, or, like Mr. B., refuse to acknowledge the problems with the other partner in a troubled marriage. With that greater understanding, the lawyer may be in a better position to counsel his client and work toward a resolution of the issues in the divorce.

It is worthwhile to explore in a little more depth the similarity between the lawyer's role and the therapist's role and the potential pitfalls of mishandling the relationships with the divorcing parties, particularly in the context of high-conflict divorce.

HIGH-CONFLICT DIVORCE

The level of conflict that occurs in divorces, like many things in life, appears to be distributed along a "bell curve." For those of you who have forgotten (or avoided) your training in statistics, you need only think of a graph showing that there are, for example, very few people who are four feet tall (one end of the graph) and very few people who are seven feet tall (the other end of the graph), but many people who are 5½ feet tall (the middle of the graph). Similarly, at the extreme low end of the divorce conflict level graph, it is a very small group of couples who are able to simply acknowledge that they have grown apart and swiftly and amicably develop a plan for dividing assets, for financial supporting children or the spouse who may need it, and for a child custody schedule that takes into account the needs of the children and the parties' skills and availability. Most couples—those in the middle of the conflict graph—have a significant degree of conflict, including arguments between themselves, negotiations between attorneys, and perhaps an appearance or two in court but eventually work out an agreed resolution.

Finally, at the other extreme end of the conflict graph, there is a small group of couples who have a very high degree of conflict, fighting over nearly every issue, taking many of those issues to court, and litigating over a long period of time. If children are involved, these parties may go back to court repeatedly for modification of child support or child custody. Lawyers spend very little time with first group of low or no-conflict people, perhaps simply drawing up the agreement the parties have reached between themselves. Lawyers, and judges, spend a lot of time with the last group of people. This last group of people has a higher percentage of individuals with personality disorders than is found in the general population, making them particularly challenging for lawyers and judges who may have no training in handling the psychodynamic reactions of these litigants or their own reactions to them.

There are a number of factors that determine the level of conflict that may be experienced in a particular case. There may be structural factors that make conflict more or less likely—whether the parties have already physically separated, how much money is at stake, the ease with which assets can be valued and incomes can be determined, whether there are children involved, and so on. One of the biggest factors, however, is the personality dynamics of each of the parties. Sometimes other relatives, particularly parents of the parties, and even friends can influence the level of conflict, leading to the "tribal warfare" described by Dr. Ehrlich. Another major factor is the approach taken by each of the lawyers. Rather than modeling healthy conflict resolution, the lawyers themselves can create additional conflict. Lawyers may take on the views of their clients and even exaggerate the clients' views. By their behavior, lawyers can teach their clients to be more combative and accusatory.

As pointed out by Dr. Ehrlich (citing Coates and Fieldstone, 2008), high-conflict cases, while a small percentage of the total number of divorce cases, are ones that take up an inordinate amount of lawyers' and courts' time and resources. Therefore, any improvements in how lawyers or judges deal with high-conflict litigants can have a large and positive ripple effect on our court system.

THE LAWYER'S ROLE AS COUNSELOR

The lawyer's role can be conceptualized like the therapist's role as described by Dr. Ehrlich. Part of the lawyer's role may be to help the client tolerate ambivalence and recognize both the positive and negative features of the marital relationship and the marital partner. Just as Dr. Ehrlich describes a "common countertransference acting out in terms of therapists allying themselves with one side of their patients' ambivalence and thus failing to facilitate its resolution or, even more problematically, contributing to a rigidifying of defense," lawyers may ally themselves with one side of their clients' feelings toward their former partners—for example, their client's expressed hatred toward their former partners. In doing so, lawyers may exacerbate the conflict. On the other hand, if the lawyer helps the client to recognize the positive aspects of the former partner's behavior—for instance, that the partner is a good parent, that the partner has been cooperative in providing information or interim financial support, and so on—the lawyer may help to reduce the level of conflict.

Just as therapists may get sucked into their client's perspectives, lawyers may. Dr. Ehrlich describes the therapist who, convinced by his patient's portrayal of the patient's wife as suffering from borderline personality disorder and of himself as an excellent parent, writes a letter to the court in support of his patient's claim for primary physical custody. The therapist erred in making a custody recommendation without conducting a full evaluation and without evaluating the mother. The therapist did not recognize the need to get a more complete data set that included information from both sides. Lawyers generally begin by getting one side of the story, but the responsible lawyer will do what he or she can to get the other side of the story, if for no other reason than the fact that the judge will make a determination after hearing the other side and the outcome can be better predicted with knowledge of the other side. Although our American legal system is built on the idea that lawyers should be "advocates" for a particular party's position, and when lawyers are in court, they may give a one-sided portrayal of facts, lawyers also have a role as "counselors," who need to look at the complete picture.[1] As counselors, lawyers need to help their clients see the complete picture, including the positive attributes and actions of their partners and their own negative attributes and actions.

As pointed out by Dr. Ehrlich, it is not always the case that a divorcing party has an unduly negative view of his or her partner; idealization of the partner also can be a problem for therapists and divorce lawyers. Lawyers may have clients who refuse to acknowledge the bad conduct of their spouses or even abuse committed by their partners, and who are extremely reluctant to leave destructive relationships. If the other party is the one seeking the divorce, the client may put his or her head in the sand and refuse to acknowledge the reality of the divorce. The party in denial may continue to insist that the partner does not really want a divorce or may blame the partner's attorney for any hostile positions taken by the partner rather than acknowledging the negative conduct of the partner. The lawyer's task in those cases may be to help the client develop a more objective view of the partner that includes his or her negative attributes and actions.

ADDING CHILDREN TO THE MIX

Separations or divorces where there are children involved are particularly difficult not just because of the extra level of emotion involved and because of the potential fallout for the children, but because it is difficult to put a price on the issues at stake. While the parties might be able to determine the economic value of the assets in dispute or of the financial support in dispute, it is not so easy to put a price tag on the well-being of one's children or on the relationship between a parent and child. Also, in cases involving children, the parents must continue to interact with one another. Each interaction is an opportunity for conflict. Moreover, the parties are likely to need to continue interacting with one another for the rest of their lives or their children's lives. Although the courts may no longer have jurisdiction once the children reach age eighteen, the parties will still need to deal with issues like where the children will go during their breaks from college or during holidays, meeting new romantic partners, children's weddings, and the births of and milestone events for grandchildren. For all of the reasons above, a lawyer is remiss if he or she ratchets up the conflict level in custody disputes between parents rather than helping his or her client to take a more objective, problem-solving approach toward resolution of the disputes.

In more extreme high-conflict cases, lawyers may contribute to a parent's alienation or estrangement from his or her children. As Dr. Ehrlich said, high-conflict divorces are "potentially treacherous because clinicians working with the high-conflict divorce are extremely vulnerable to committing clinical blunders and ethical transgressions unless they understand well the forces they are dealing with." High-conflict divorces are similarly treacherous for lawyers. If the lawyer simply accepts a parent's negative characterization of the other parent without looking for supporting evidence and while dismissing the evidence to the contrary, then the lawyer may ultimately be doing his or her client, and the profession, a disservice. On the other side, if a lawyer simply blames the other parent for alienating the child against his client and refuses to acknowledge how his or her client's own conduct has affected the child's thoughts and feelings, that lawyer is remiss. In either case, the lawyer's conduct may contribute to deterioration in the child or children's relationships with one or both parents and increase the emotional stress suffered by everyone in the process—children, parents, lawyers, and judge.

BEWARE THE TRANSFERENCE AND
COUNTERTRANSFERENCE REACTIONS

Parties not only "seek confirmation of their views of the bad character of the spouse and vindication of their own behaviors and character" from therapists, as pointed out by Dr. Ehrlich, they seek the same confirmation and vindication from their lawyers. Any suggestion by the lawyer that the spouse may not be behaving as badly as claimed is taken as a sign of disloyalty from the lawyer as is any suggestion that the client may have behaved incorrectly. The lawyers, like the therapists, "will face their patient's disdain, if not outright rage, if they do not accept that person's views of the divorce, including the harsh assessment of the ex-spouse." Clients may engage in splitting, distortion, and delusional projection with their lawyers just as they do with their therapists.

It may be difficult for lawyers to control their own reactions to these and other difficult client behaviors. It is important for lawyers to remember that, as stated by Dr. Ehrlich, their clients may be acting badly because of early losses or narcissistic traumas and/or because "the losses and narcissistic injuries that in here in divorce are, essentially, more than they can manage psychically." If this is understood, the lawyer may be able to summon greater empathy for the client rather than giving in to a visceral negative reaction. The lawyer may realize, for example, that his client is not necessarily consciously distorting the truth; rather, the client's statements may be a manifestation of psychological phenomenon—defenses—that serve the purpose in the individual of avoiding psychic pain. In other words, the client is suffering to some extent. In addition, the lawyer may need to recognize that his or her reactions to the client may not be purely objective but may be influenced by his or her own psychodynamic makeup, including his or her own losses and narcissistic traumas.

CONCLUSION

There are probably few, if any, children who grow up saying that they want to be divorce lawyers. However, some people who become divorce lawyers recognize that as divorce lawyers, they have the opportunity to help people through what might be the most difficult time in their lives. These lawyers also may see that they have the opportunity to help make people better parents and co-parents. In helping parents to resolve custody cases in an amicable fashion, lawyers can have a dramatic impact on children's lives.

One of the best ways for lawyers to practice "therapeutic jurisprudence" and minimize the negative psychological sequelae of divorce while maximizing the positive psychological sequelae is to reduce the conflict level in their cases. How can the lawyer reduce conflict in divorce? Some prescriptions may be easy and obvious—for example, don't write the nasty letter that is full of adjectives, opinions, and hominem attacks and short on nouns and facts. However, other prescriptions require more work and study. Some suggestions are provided in Anderer and Glass's (2000) paper, "A Therapeutic Jurisprudence and Preventive Law Approach to Family Law."

In addition, lawyers could stand to educate themselves about psychodynamic phenomena so that they are more thoughtful in evaluating information from their clients and better able to recognize distortions in that information. Lawyers also need to understand their own reactions to their clients so that they can better counsel them. Similarly, as they attempt to reduce conflict, judges could benefit from a greater understanding of psychodynamic factors affecting the litigants that appear before them and affecting the judges themselves.

As suggested at the outset, the psychodynamic factors that are at work among the various people in our divorce legal system are worthy of further and careful scrutiny so that we can better train lawyers and judges to reduce conflict. As the parent of three daughters who are now teenagers/young adults, I think about what I would want the process to be if, heaven forbid, my daughters needed to go through it. I certainly hope that if that day should ever come, the process is one that is more therapeutic in that it minimizes the negative psychological sequelae for them and promotes positive psychological sequelae.

NOTE

1. No less a figure than Abraham Lincoln gave the following advice to lawyers: "Discourage litigation. Persuade your neighbors to compromise whenever you can. Point out to them how the nominal winner is often a real loser—in fees, expenses, and waste of time. As a peacemaker the lawyer has a superior opportunity of being a good man. There will still be business enough." To the list of litigation costs we should add emotional angst.

Chapter Six

Stories from the Edge

Divorce as Redemption

Elizabeth H. Thomas

Growing up in rural Virginia, I never knew anyone who had been divorced. The concept was completely alien. I knew of families that faced difficult, sometimes extraordinary, circumstances. The Marshalls had that drunkard of a father. Mr. Jones was not quite right in the head. And the whole Spencer clan was inconsolable since little Charlie drowned in the pond. Growing up, I was familiar with misfortune, but not with divorce. This small community, so forgiving, held many varieties of family, but none included divorce.

I say this by way of context and how the American marriage and divorce landscape has changed over the last half a century or more. My community in rural Virginia was not so uncommon several decades ago. Now, things are different.

Marriage is less the norm than in years past. There are more recognized couple arrangements, such as cohabitation outside of marriage, same-sex couples, even what are known as "registered agreements" in some European countries. In the United States, when people do choose to marry, they are generally older than in the past. Childbearing outside of marriage is more accepted. While marriage has taken a diminished status, people continue to operate in variable family units. Today there are blended families, mixed race families, offspring born through in vitro fertilization, open adoption, and all manner of nontraditional arrangements.

Divorce has changed as well. Statistically, divorce rates have actually declined in recent years. This might suggest a trend toward greater family stability. Or, more likely, it is a consequence of the numbers. With fewer "official" marriages come fewer "official" divorces.

Because of various constellations of families within and without marriage in the present culture, the idea of "divorce" can seem outdated. Perhaps it is more accurate to think of couples that come apart as "separations" or "un-couplings." These terms are broader and take in a greater number of situations. But after all the parsing of terms, in the end, the concern is about adult couple relationships coming apart. Whatever the terms, whatever the statistics, what matters is that families come undone. It is, after all, not the numbers so much as the impact.

Unhappiness in couples can lead to psychological difficulties as well as poor physical health, showing up in higher levels of cardiovascular disease, diabetes, obesity, and other health concerns, including life expectancy. When relationships flounder, there can be significant public cost. Conversely, a strong marriage or partnership, in addition to a sense of general well-being, can lengthen and even save lives.

Partnerships in distress impact children, and this is a major public health concern. Some of the distress of the adult relationship shows up in children as psychological and physical problems, including poor school performance, heightened levels of anxiety, clinical depression, obesity, and antisocial behavior. Public social services are hard-pressed to address the problems at their roots, relying instead on such child-focused interventions such as psychotropic medication or parenting classes. While these measures may prove useful to some degree, they generally fail to address the underlying problems. The vast, cumbersome environment of social services can work against deeper dimensions of assistance, by enabling an "audit culture" to direct interventions (Lawlor, 2012). As reported in Great Britain, but relevant for the United States, this ethos,

> with its prioritization of the evaluation of performance outcomes at the expense of considering the processes by which these outcomes are achieved, can provide psychological escape mechanisms for staff at all levels to avoid the pain and difficulty of face-to-face front line social work with disturbed families. (Balfour, Morgan, & Vincent, 2012, pp. xxxv–xxxvi)

Time-limited, measureable interventions can offer benefits, but they generally leave unattended the deeper relationship issues that are at the heart of real change.

Even where there is a focus on the children in social service settings, the importance of the parental couple can be overlooked. While social services target children and the family, what is missing is attention to the couple. The quality of the relationship of the parents can impact the whole family.

Troubled couple relationships are the precursor to separation and divorce. Intervention is needed at the point of the couple in distress because help at this point can improve the well-being of the adults themselves and establish a firm base for children. Intervention at the couple level serves to strengthen individuals and families, and to provide healthful transitions in the event of ultimate separation.

Today, with the centrality of social media, the emphasis is on immediacy and ease of change—click here to get the lowest mortgage rates, or sign on to lose 10 pounds in three days! The culture expects immediate rewards and, consequently, favors impulsive actions over considered decisions. These societal forces do not support meaningful and effective treatment for couple relationships.

What follows are stories about couple relationships on the edge of divorce, and our work together, work grounded in psychoanalytically informed couple therapy. This, I believe, is the most effective intervention and offers the best hope for healing when relationships rupture. Before introducing the protagonists of these stories, I'd like to lay some theoretical groundwork.

THEORETICAL GROUNDWORK

Some key concepts in work with couples have to do with notions of containment and containers; thirds and triangles; projective and introjective processes; and capacity for such things as mentalization, self-reflection, and creativity. Achievement and deficit in terms of developmental maturation is also relevant, such as whether or not the individuals have been able to give up early narcissism in favor of true intimacy with another, and to mourn the inevitable losses on the way to maturity. These elements help guide work with couples, whether the outcome is a stronger partnership or separation and divorce.

A basic question in work with adult couples is whether and how the partnership is working. Conceptually, we can ask, is the relationship able to function as a container? And if not, why not?

The idea of a psychological container was first introduced by Wilfred Bion (1962), who spoke of a two-person, container-contained dynamic characterizing the mother–infant relationship. It is an idea similar to, but different from, Winnicott's (1960) concept of "holding." Both concepts have to do with the maternal environment. Both use terminology that suggests boundaries, safety, and care.

Writing in the context of marriage, but with application to any committed adult couple relationship, Warren Colman (1993) introduced the concept of a "marital container." Colman says:

> The *relationship itself* becomes the container, the creative outcome of the couple's union, to which both partners can relate. It is an image of something the couple are continually in the process of creating, sustaining, and maintaining,

while at the same time feeling that they exist within it—are contained by it. When couples talk of "our relationship," it is this image they refer to—something that is felt to exist independently of them and yet to which both are required to contribute. (pp. 89–90)

Thus the question—is the relationship able to function as a container?—highlights the presence and operation of a third entity. There are not only two individual adults in the picture but also the vital, if somewhat elusive, "relationship." In a strong partnership, the inevitable tensions that beset even the most agreeable couple get worked out. It may take some time and it may not be easy, but there is a structure that allows disturbance without breakage. Conflict can be managed within the containing walls of the relationship. Thus, the idea of a marital container—or what might more appropriately be called a *relational* container—is useful in work with couples.

Somewhat different ideas, formulated from work with individuals in psychoanalysis, have been set forth by Ron Britton (1989) and Jessica Benjamin (2004). Britton noticed a tight, vise-like experience with some patients, and an atmosphere controlled by the patient as an emotional tyrant. There was no space, not even to think. It was a situation defined by and ruled by opposites.

Britton noticed this severe constraint in contrast to what he designated as "triangular space," a psychic environment in which we can see ourselves in interaction with others. Out of constriction, Britton proposed a "third position," from which we can observe and be observed. We can think our own thoughts as well as those of others, even if they offer a different point of view. We can be in conversation with a true other. Thoughts of more than one person, brought together, allow for creative expression and the possibility of the emergence of something new. In other words, Britton maintains, there can be intercourse, extending a biological ability into a symbolic capacity.

Jessica Benjamin writes of a similar problem of constricted psychic space and finds a solution in what she names "the third." Whereas Britton noticed how one position relies on its opposite for its very existence, Benjamin saw how one position relies for its existence on a complement. It is a small but important distinction. For Britton, the opposites he recognized fell into splits reminiscent of Melanie Klein's paranoid/schizoid position such as good and bad, right and wrong. All were either black or white, no gray. Exact opposites require tenacity to stay exact; something in between is just no good and pressure to give a little only encourages extension into the outer reaches of opposite poles. This is particularly relevant for work with couples because polarization is such a familiar presentation.

Benjamin, on the other hand, makes note of complementarities, such as up and down, like the action of a seesaw, where one position relies on its complement not for existence but for function. For Benjamin, complementarities are not so much exact opposites—linguistically or existentially—as relational qualities. Thus, she introduces the idea of "doer" and its complement, "done to." The resulting relational impasse finds solution in "thirdness."

Finally, Mary Morgan (2005) takes up Britton's ideas and applies them to couple therapy, with the notion of the creative couple and the creative couple state of mind. Morgan explains that

> the "creative couple" is primarily a psychic development, one in which it is possible to allow different thoughts and feelings to come together in one's mind, and for something to develop out of them. (p. 22)

She goes on to explain that

> the creative couple state of mind allows for ambivalence and the toleration of the inevitability of conflict and tension. This is the kind of relationship in which creative solutions are sometimes possible—solutions that neither of the individuals would have imagined or found on their own. (pp. 29–30)

So these theoretical concepts begin to come together: containment, thirds and triangles, capacity, and ultimately something beyond the obvious that has to be created within relationship. These ideas, drawn from psychoanalytic work with individuals, are efforts to conceptualize the complex, multilayered, and often furiously paced world of relationship. It is to these ideas that the therapist can appeal for some notion of how and to what end the therapeutic work can bend.

MR. AND MRS. QUINN, PART I

Mr. and Mrs. Quinn, an immigrant couple in their forties, were on the brink of divorce. Despite being married and having three children—external evidence of an adult relationship—Mr. and Mrs. Quinn were not able to function as a "creative couple." When the relationship was strained, there was little resiliency to carry them through and so, separation/divorce threatened.

Today, Mr. and Mrs. Quinn are telling me about their lunch at a trendy café, Mr. Quinn's suggestion. Their account follows a familiar format: Mr. Quinn makes appeals for recognition—"how did you like the salad?"—while Mrs. Quinn swipes away his overtures like so many crumbs—"it's okay, not great." Discovery of Mr. Quinn's affair, now ended, brought them into treatment. Mrs. Quinn has been playing the injured party ceaselessly, a role she knows well and refines exquisitely, its roots in a childhood full of betrayal. It is an exquisite example of Benjamin's (2004) "doer" and "done-to," where Mr. Quinn is the "doer" and Mrs. Quinn is the one "done to." For his part,

Mr. Quinn agilely tacks back and forth between wretched adulterer and an ordinary man, full of rage. Despite the drama this day, I find myself bored. It seems that the therapy has wrung itself into a tight, twisted rag, good for nothing more than to wipe off a sticky lunch counter.

Mr. Quinn makes an effort—several, in fact. He selects a very nice café for lunch and he shows interest in Mrs. Quinn's opinion of the food. He seems to want to connect. He makes a bid, but Mrs. Quinn turns away. Already we have a micro moment of disconnect, of "uncoupleness." What I mean by this is that while Mr. and Mrs. Quinn appear to be together as a couple, they are not. They are like cars on a train that uncouple in order to reconfigure the purpose of the journey. They are not connected to something greater than themselves.

As I watch and listen to Mr. and Mrs. Quinn, I am missing evidence of their marriage as a "container." That has been my impression all along. Today is no different. They seem alone, operating like two single, disconnected entities with no third influence to which they can appeal.

Mr. Quinn goes on, making banal advances—"I'm trying to connect with you"; Mrs. Quinn, averting her eyes, is spiteful—"you spoil it, always." Parry; riposte. Now it's like a fencing match, only less elegant. This couple cannot see one another. They cannot reach one another, and the breach seems to be widening.

I begin to ponder my boredom. It occurs to me that I am holding a more complex experience, one involving impotence, helplessness, of being invisible, all feelings shared by the three of us in this sad little consulting room. I am reminded of Mr. Quinn's feelings of impotence in particular. His efforts to connect with Mrs. Quinn this day are rebuffed, like they are on so many occasions. Over and over, the food he offers—the love he offers—is rejected. He carries a constant burden of failure. Even in their sexual life, Mr. Quinn comes up short, unable to sustain an erection. And they both feel betrayed.

Interestingly, the disappointment of sexual performance is, for Mrs. Quinn, also a kind of victory. It fuels both her sense of outrage—one more example of her husband's inadequacy—and her self need for rectitude. Her history includes an unavoidable but traumatic childhood separation from her mother, and multiple instances of infidelity on the part of her father, finally resulting in the parents' divorce. The oldest of four, Mrs. Quinn was tasked with caring for her younger siblings, a job she took on vigorously but repeatedly came up short because of her youth and inexperience. Circumstances repeatedly overwhelmed her abilities and she was left too often feeling a pulsing helplessness. There was so much to do for so small a child. Thus, if others fail, then she stands a chance of recovering the moral high road. Perhaps she figures it is worth it to suffer if doing so brings someone else down. It is a sadomasochistic drive very tightly constructed, and resonant in the couple relationship through projective and introjective processes.

This current exercise in couple therapy, in fact, was set up by Mrs. Quinn as punishment for Mr. Quinn's infidelity. Since he erred, he must pay by going to couple therapy, among other things. Mr. Quinn hates coming to couple therapy, and I feel complicit in the ruse. I feel not only used, but a dolt, too stupid to realize that the treatment is a farce. But I carry on, in the belief that perhaps I am not totally useless and perhaps something can come of this. I also seek consultation with a more experienced colleague. It seems I need containment myself.

Impotence and helplessness pervade the atmosphere, along with an unnerving and contradictory sense of victory and conquest. Here there are winners and losers, "doer" and "done to." This, together with the arrangement of the therapy just noted, sets out an atmosphere of traps, vises with no escape. It is difficult, if not impossible at times, to think. Much like a frightened animal in the sights of a predator, my mind freezes in the interest of survival. That must contribute to my boredom as well, my mind just shutting down. I see before me two adults, but I feel as though I'm dealing with two contrary toddlers. Maybe that's the clue. I consider myself caught in a narcissistic organization.

As mentioned earlier, concepts of thirds seek to provide a solution to interpersonal narcissistic binds. The understanding that another perspective emanates from a wholly other subjective world is both terrifying and hopeful. Terrifying because it involves giving up an old way of seeing the world, one that is familiar and relatively simple since it only involves one subject—me and my wishes. It is a world thought to be idyllic even if it was relationally unsatisfying. Hopeful because the world and the opportunities therein expand, and while the future is unknown, the belief in goodness overcomes prior persecutory anxieties. It is the movement from Klein's (1940) paranoid/schizoid position to the depressive position.

Despite the cumbersome language, the passage into adulthood involves giving up narcissism and omnipotence, and mourning the loss. Only then can a person engage in a world of other human beings, where one sees the other and is seen by the other, where one is capable of and can expect mutual recognition. Reality may be difficult, but at least one is not in it alone.

Finally, on this day, what might I make of this feeling of invisibility? While related to the aforementioned reflections—triangular arrangements, narcissism and omnipotence, mourning and achievement of mature relating—there was something else, a refinement, in having a sense of not being seen. If I give voice to my thoughts, I am ignored. Mr. and Mrs. Quinn talk right over me. If I remain quiet and retreat into myself for some relief, I am attacked, as though my mere physical presence is an insult.

In one of our early sessions, Mrs. Quinn accused me of being in cahoots with Mr. Quinn, believing that I was allowing his adulterous behavior to go unchallenged. She had claimed, loudly, that I was too easy on him, that I needed to "call it like it is!" If she saw me at all, it was as a weak, useless sycophant, or a wet rag. In one way, though, Mr. Quinn and I were in league. We both felt not "good enough" despite our best efforts. We both came up short, recipients of Mrs. Quinn's projected insecurities. Or that was the role we had been playing. Her background suggested as much.

As I sit with this couple every week, it feels impossible to help. My observations have no impact; my comments seem to skittle off the surface like water on a hot griddle. We are all hopelessly abandoned. Mrs. Quinn was abandoned as a child, having been (unavoidably) denied contact with her mother. Mr. Quinn is abandoned in his efforts to appease, all of which fall into a black hole. And I feel abandoned by the couple. Our feelings seem to pool around a sense of feeling unworthy, perhaps this couples' shared unconscious belief of not being "good enough," with the accompanying and understandable rage. Both Mr. and Mrs. Quinn are rageful, defensive, attacking, while I look on helplessly.

This is a sad story, but it is not uncommon. We can wonder: What are the prospects for resolution of this couple's problems? Would medication help? Would homework exercises bring them closer together? Would they benefit from sex therapy? Should their children be brought in for family sessions? I don't know what to do, really. We'll just have to see.

PAUL AND IRENE

This is a story about Paul, a 55-year-old African American, and his wife, Irene. I see Paul in individual treatment. I have always had in mind that Paul is part of a couple. Even when he talks about very personal details of his life, there is another human presence that is part of him. It's hard to pinpoint what it is exactly that conveys this impression, but even if Paul had never mentioned his wife, I would have had a notion of her. I know of Irene only through Paul's eyes and what he chooses to relate to me.

I do not understand Paul and Irene to represent a "creative couple." This idea of a developmental achievement, wherein the relationship involves three entities—the self, the partner, *and* the relationship—is in contrast to the primary relationship of mother and baby (Morgan, 2012). However, I do think that Paul brings to the marriage many of the qualities that contribute to a mature couple relationship, such as an appreciation for the relationship itself as a vital component, a sense of both autonomy and dependency, relinquishment of grandiosity, and acceptance of reality. So while this is not a story of divorce, it is antecedent to an unknown future. Whether that involves suspension in an emotional desert, divorce, or development of a marriage of true depth and intimacy, is not known, but we can wonder about all of these possible outcomes.

Paul began a recent session recounting two disasters: the cistern had broken and the car battery had died. He spoke first of the cistern, describing a great swooshing sound in the middle of the night that he had first believed to be the collapse of the sewage treatment plant up the hill from their home. But it was not sewage that overtook the house; rather, it was water and a lot of it. The following morning, Paul was able to find a local contractor to rebuild the cistern, but it was going to take a long time—maybe a month or six weeks. Paul and Irene had resigned themselves to making do.

When the car wouldn't start, a workman from the cistern project charged the battery and warned, "Don't turn it off! Go straight to Ricky's for a new one." Paul and Irene went to Ricky's but had to wait in line a long time before finally getting to the clerk who, after a slow-drip trip to the back, returned to report that they did not have the battery in stock. Meanwhile, the car was kept running. Paul and Irene then drove to another shop where they were met by what Paul described as "a small, brusque woman" behind the counter. She, too, disappeared into the back and soon announced that yes, they had it. Relieved, Paul wrote a check on the spot, but when he went outside to install the battery, he was surprised to see that the little woman had already taken care of it. Delighted, Paul thanked the woman profusely, and gave her a big tip. He and Irene were good to go!

Paul's life could be described as a string of disasters, the two he reported in the session being only the most recent. He grew up an only child in an alcoholic family where violence was common. His mother often hit him, beat him, and threatened God's wrath if he misbehaved. For Paul, God was a harsh, vengeful God that ruled the universe with punishments for every conceivable misdeed, or so that was the home atmosphere. Paul strove to be good and to please God. He even became a minister in his Fundamentalist faith in an effort to appease the dual gods of mother and the Old Testament. He has since, however, renounced his faith.

When bad things happen, Paul typically reacts with fear, anxious that he is somehow responsible. When the great swoosh came in the middle of the night, Paul's first thought was of being taken over by "shit." His life, after all, was one awash in shit—from this moment of something terrible happening all the way back to his childhood when life was lived amid the sloppiness and squalor of alcoholism, together with a family atmosphere that was out of control and terrifying.

Then, almost simultaneously, Paul allowed himself to hold off on that disaster in order to take in the reality of the actual disaster, the cistern. This is new. The old paranoia is there in the first, brief assessment, but it doesn't take over. There is room to think and to assess the real situation. The cistern broke, not the sewage treatment plant. This is symbolically relevant as well. While shit happens, Paul is not necessarily the one responsible. His tone in relaying this part of the story to me was almost giddy, as though he were in the midst of an epiphany in the telling. He was realizing at that moment that stuff happens, but it doesn't mean he's responsible or that he must atone. He tells me, "Look, things happen, you just don't know. You do what you can and move on. There's no big God up there sending down thunderbolts. Look, we've been to the moon. No God. To deep space. No God. So maybe there's no one in charge of the universe. Not God. Not me."

The cistern breaks. This great container has burst open, sending a flood of water over Paul and Irene, like a baptism? Perhaps, but more likely to my ear, the cistern represents the failed container of the marriage. While this couple has been together for twenty plus years, the relationship lacks mutuality. There is no abuse, nothing objectionable really. It's just ho-hum, with no spark, no life. It's kind of like a dead battery.

Help for the car comes by way of one of the workers on the cistern, so Paul has wasted no time getting that first project under way. Paul and Irene drive around in search of a new battery. There are things we can't see, that are in the "back." The right thing may or may not be there but eventually, the problem is solved by a small, brusque woman. Perhaps this is the therapist—a woman on the small side who doesn't say a whole lot but is viewed as brusque when she does.

Going into the "back" suggests a dark, mysterious place that not everyone is privy to. It is the unconscious. We go back through time and memory to discover artifacts that have been laying fallow for a lifetime. Paul reaches back into unconscious dimensions with the small woman, looking for something—some memory, some experience—that can be carried forward and made useful in the present. When the second clerk not only has the exact part, but installs it as well, everything begins to work properly. Paul and Irene can travel together once again, as things were reconnected and charged.

Later in the same hour, the topic turned to some of the activities that Paul and Irene do together. He described a recent outing when they went swimming in the lake. While in the water, Irene said she was cold, so Paul said that she should hug his back. She did and warmed up. When Paul turned around to embrace her, Irene grew tense and pulled away. Paul joked that Irene might have to get comfortable with embracing and kissing in public. He said that they were, after all, married.

Paul invites Irene to embrace his back, a practical suggestion but one tinged with longing and desire. It may be the only way Paul can get Irene to embrace him until he is able to turn around. They see not eye-to-eye, but rather in a more primitive state of skin-to-skin, like a neonate with its mother immediately after birth. While Paul and Irene are skin-to-skin, all is well, but turning to a more mature meeting of adults eye-to-eye, the relationship experiences distancing by Irene. This is another disaster for Paul. He wants an adult relationship but Irene seems to be capable only of a primary relationship like that between mother and child. But armed with his newly developed acceptance of "things happen," Paul is able to tolerate the disappointment, cajoling Irene to accept the reality of their marriage. In time, perhaps things will improve, he said. He has seen change in himself, so there's hope for Irene as well. He remains deeply ambivalent about there being a God, whatever, whoever that might be, but he has hope. He knows something about love. He knows something about trust and having Irene's back. He says he is committed to his relationship with Irene. He says he will just wait and see what happens.

MR. AND MRS. QUINN, PART 2

The work with Mr. and Mrs. Quinn continued with each one's conviction that the other was to blame for the problems in the marriage. I continued to worry about how to help them. I continued to seek consultation. Gradually, change grew in the psychological environment. The Quinns seemed more relaxed, less pressured. They laughed together. It was more laughing *with* than laughing *at*. There was less urgency in the quest for answers. I, too, felt more at ease and began to look more carefully at the couple before me.

Then Mrs. Quinn, who had been having some health issues, was diagnosed with Parkinson's disease. The two were shaken by this news. As doctors' appointments piled up and worry intensified, the couple moved forward with resolve, steady, and sober. Mr. Quinn freed up his work schedule to accompany Mrs. Quinn to her doctors' appointments. Mrs. Quinn sought out friends in the health field for consultation and arranged second opinions. They checked in with each other about each day's activities and how they were managing emotionally. Their children were told the situation and pitched in to help.

One day, Mrs. Quinn mentioned that her in-laws were in town for a visit. She then began to advocate forcefully for Mr. Quinn to talk to his mother about their situation and how it was affecting him. She said that he was under a lot of stress and, since Mr. Quinn and his mother were close, confiding in her would be a good thing.

Silently, I understood that Mrs. Quinn wanted to help her husband, to provide a support for him. The medical picture was a confusion of recommendations—for medications, for procedures—together with conflicting predictions on the progress of the disease. There were a lot of unknowns.

Sensitive to the increasing stress that this caused, Mrs. Quinn hoped to provide some relief for her husband. She wanted to expand the support system for Mr. Quinn, within the trusted confines of the family. It seemed a good idea.

But Mr. Quinn would have none of it. He explained that while he loved his mother, he did not have "that kind of relationship" with her. He did not want to talk to her about this. In fact, he said, "I don't really talk to her about things that much." At this, Mrs. Quinn declared aggressively, "What?! You talk to her all the time, like every day!" This challenge seemed remarkably like the old refrain, full of absolutes. I realized I was holding my breath, preparing for submersion.

Mr. Quinn, unwavering, complied and countered, "Not every day." Then he elaborated: "I talk to her probably once a week. You know how ill my father is and a lot falls to her. I want to support her, to be there to help in any way I can. They live so far away. It's the least I can do from here."

Mrs. Quinn persisted with her own perspective while revealing a part of her own vulnerability and needs. "But she could listen to you," she insisted. "I'll probably have enough to worry about just keeping my own self together." She says this with a little laugh, but the seriousness is clear. Mrs. Quinn wants to make sure her husband is taken care of and that any stress he bears will not weigh on her. She has enough.

Both Mr. and Mrs. Quinn share their worries and their ideas about how things might be addressed. Despite Mrs. Quinn's edging into an argument, both are sharing ideas and, more important, revealing tender parts of themselves. They both are frightened—about Mrs. Quinn's diagnosis, about their ability to cope, about each others' commitment to a common pledge, "in sickness and in health." They keep the conversation going, deepening the exchange.

He says, "If I need to talk to someone, I want it to be someone of my own choosing. And not my mother. I don't want to have it all set up that I talk to my mother. I don't know what I'll feel like. Maybe I'll be fine and won't need to talk to anyone … but if I do, I want to think about who that should be … actually, I might be comfortable talking to Sam, or to Frank, he's been through this with his wife's cancer. I'd be comfortable talking to either of them more than my mother."

Mr. Quinn demonstrates so much in this statement: increasing clarity about his own needs, ability to tolerate not knowing, unwillingness to foreclose on possibility, thinking and reflection. Mrs. Quinn, too, is able to set forth her own feelings of vulnerability, alongside her caring for Mr. Quinn. They listen to each other and respond, taking in what the other has said, weighing it, and offering a next step. It was like the two were driving down an expansive street, full of possibility. With the approach of a roundabout, they did not need to stop before turning in the right direction, they could keep moving toward their intended destination. If they missed the exit, then they could keep going and pick it up on the next round. With this turn in the treatment, it was evident that Mr. and Mrs. Quinn were on their way, equipped to redeem their relationship.

This was a hopeful and hoped for outcome. Their understanding of each other and mutual respect could be a foundation for future cooperation. They could turn to the marriage itself to function creatively in the interest of the couple. If they were to stay together, the marriage would be a sturdy enough container to manage future of ups and downs. With enhanced intimacy and trustworthiness, and with a capacity to arrive at creative solutions, Mr. and Mrs. Quinn could rightly be said to have become a creative couple. They transformed "doer" and "done to" into "do-able."

CONCLUDING REMARKS

From these stories, there emerge some constituents of healthy couple relationships and the difficulties that emerge when these elements are absent. Concepts such as whether or not the marriage/relationship functions as a container, so that during times of strain the relationship itself can serve as a resource for the couple. It is useful to learn whether and to what extent the couple operates within a marital/relational triangle, with capacities for being both included and excluded. What measure of trust characterizes the relationship? And to what degree has each relinquished narcissism and been able to mourn that loss? How has the couple handled loss generally, including each person's ability to mourn? These are significant indicators of a couple's functioning and inform a prognosis should treatment be undertaken, whether the desired outcome is for a renewed and strengthened relationship or for separation. If the latter is the outcome, then these same capacities can be enlisted for a constructive transition.

I think working psychoanalytically is analogous to what art students practice in order to learn about perspective. In a class on drawing, the student is instructed to draw the negative space. This means to draw not the object indicated; rather, to draw the space around the object. It may seem like the same thing, but it's not. The student's perspective changes. When asked to draw the negative space, the person drawing must look at the thing differently, in a new way, and try to give shape to that new thing. Similarly, the therapist can see the couple and hear the report of their difficulties and other objective data. With a psychoanalytic stance, the therapist looks at the edge, as it were, of what is overt to try and determine the architecture of the psychic space.

This is accomplished by attending to what's just beyond the edge of the presentation. For the clinician, this may be using countertransference and taking one's own thoughts and feelings as information. For evaluating the couple situation, it may mean unpacking a suspected projection as defense. For example, someone presents as very bold and confident while the partner presents as meek and insecure, as suggested in the story of Mr. and Mrs. Quinn. Is this the true picture? Or might the opposite be more true? What does it look like if the roles are reversed? We look a little closer and consider what's just beyond the apparent. While it may not be obvious at first, the clues to our understanding may lie just beyond the edge.

This was the case with Mr. and Mrs. Quinn. So much of what was informative was on the edge—the countertransference, the thoughts and feelings of the therapist, projections, personal history. By looking with an eye to the negative space, we may create the same picture as someone else who is drawing the object, but we have done so from a different perspective. Working with psychoanalytic principles changes the perspective by emphasizing unconscious processes active between the couple and within the couple relationship—and, of course, in the engagement with the therapist.

The language of psychoanalysis is cumbersome—"projective identification," "objects," "countertransference," and so on. That is why we so often recall antiquity, those reservoirs of universal truth already mastered in myth, Greek drama, and even fairy tales. We struggle to convey our understanding of unconscious processes with words that often leave us feeling not so much enlightened as incompetent. That is why we reach for metaphor not only to convey but also to inform our understanding of deep human experiences.

In the story of Mr. and Mrs. Quinn, food/the salad was a metaphor for love. For others, it might be money or time. And for Paul and Irene, the metaphor for love was a car battery! But whatever the objective thing, there is likely a dual meaning, one that is literal and allows for a cohesive story, and another that makes use of the literal as a stand-in for something else, something harder to capture in a single word. Like the art student, we see both the object and the space around the object. We hear the story and the deeper human experience beyond the story. Metaphor bends around the literal to direct our attention to something more. It is a communicative gesture wherein we seek to convey in everyday language what we understand about experience that is beyond words.

What does all this have to do with the "redemption" in this contribution's title? Perhaps it lies in our work to enhance some characteristics of mature relating outlined by Stanley Ruszczynski (2005). They are, in addition to dependence, "toleration of the loss of narcissism and omnipotence, the capacity to be included and to tolerate being excluded, knowing about one's loving and hating feelings, bearing guilt, and experiencing gratitude" (p. 33). Achievement of some or all of these fluid but unquestionably mature human relational qualities brings one out of human pain and suffering and into the light of acceptance and presence. The stories in some way are metaphors for this journey, whether ending in separation or reconciliation. In either case, achievement of human capacity, through processes involving loss and recovery, mourning and self-reflection, is the restoration of human potential and goodness. It is redemption.

Chapter Seven

On Fragments, Metaphor, and the Edge

Kathleen Ross

> Break a vase, and the love that reassembles the fragments is stronger than
> that love that took its symmetry for granted when it was whole.
>
> —Derek Walcott

Dr. Elizabeth Thomas, with vivid language and rich metaphor, has brought us
inside her consulting room and regaled us with stories of what transpires there
in her sessions with couples, or with individuals who are part of a couple. We
are privileged to share this material, to be a fly on the wall observing intimate
therapeutic encounters, and most of all to ponder along with Dr. Thomas her
own responses to the distress brought in by her patients in their search for
help. Whether couple therapy represents a substantial portion, or perhaps just
a fraction of our own practice, we can all take something of value from this
chapter and its wise, clear-eyed assessment of what it takes to work effectively with couples on the edge of destruction, despair, and divorce.

Given the existence in our present national culture of diverse family group-
ings, and the statistical decline of traditional, heterosexual marriage—the
"one man and one woman" model of a married couple—Dr. Thomas muses
that the idea of divorce may seem quaint and outmoded, an artifact of a more
rigid time when people did not have as much freedom to choose how they
wanted to live, or with whom. She argues instead for a broader concept of
uncoupling, separation, coming apart or coming undone in couple relationships. The health and strength of partnerships of all sorts, not just legally
sanctioned ones, affect the well-being of the adults and children within the
orbit of the couple at the center. Dr. Thomas reminds us that couples often
hold together families, and that by helping them either survive their difficulties intact or separate in a less hurtful way, we help many others as well.

Coming apart or coming undone are terms that effectively convey the emotional state of loss and chaos that may accompany the breakup of any couple relationship. It is my own professional and personal experience, however, that when legal proceedings become part of the uncoupling process, an extra dimension is added to the feelings of guilt, shame, betrayal, anger, and inadequacy expressed by those affected; this may be especially true when religious beliefs or doctrine are part of the mix. Likewise, the effects of a divorce that happened in a less open-minded time or place may continue to reverberate for the patients we see currently. We have gathered at today's Mahler Symposium, I believe, to talk about all these varied endings: both "official" divorce, and uncoupling and its aftermath in a broader psychic formulation, both/and, not either/or. I would also like to point out that while marriage rates are in decline for heterosexual couples, not even a year has passed since hard-won marriage equality for LGBTQ couples was expanded to all fifty of the United States. For some among us, the right to be married or divorced, far from being outmoded, has only just begun.

Dr. Thomas's portrait of her childhood in rural Virginia, where there existed all manner of human troubles but she knew no one who had been divorced, evokes a particular set of beliefs and assumptions about couples, families, and marriage. When I was growing up in post-World War II suburban New Jersey, divorce was uncommon in my world too—or so I thought. During my high school years, somehow someone around me let slip that my mother had been married and divorced before meeting my father. Approaching my younger, also teenaged brother with this new and confusing information, I asked: Did you know that Mom was married before? He replied: I knew that Dad was, but not Mom. And thus we learned that both our parents had intimate histories kept out of view, past, childless unions now ended and considered irrelevant to the present. In that time and place, such histories were not to be discussed with children, if at all.

While a wide cultural gap might lie between Dr. Thomas's rural Southern community where divorce simply didn't exist, and my Northeastern suburb where divorce occurred but wasn't openly discussed, perhaps we might draw some connections first between those two points, and from there to the illuminating cases Dr. Thomas shares with us today. In my understanding, my parents, having each endured their own difficult situations before meeting, marrying, and starting a family, wanted to wipe the slate clean and only look forward in life. In a sense, they strove to make our suburban home more like an idealized, middle-class version of Dr. Thomas's rural place, a space where we children would not know anyone who had been divorced and would only see an intact, functioning marriage. Divorce carried a stigma of shame and failure, a mistake best left behind along with the lower socioeconomic status both my parents also had known in their early lives. There was to be no edge, as Dr. Thomas calls it, of past rupture—only the smooth surface of a more fortunate present.

We need not look far to find new efforts across the United States to enforce, increasingly through restrictive and hateful laws, an idealized vision of a supposedly more certain way of life where marriage and family revert to that simple equation of one man and one woman, together as long as they both shall live. The multiple causes behind this phenomenon lie outside of my expertise or the scope of this symposium, but here, I believe, we can locate the connecting point between Dr. Thomas's childhood place, my own, and the work we do now with our patients. Divorce no longer carries the social or even religious stigma of days past, but defenses against loss and sadness, the unconscious wish for love without end, and the anger, resentment, and rage ignited when the child inside the adult feels abandoned live on despite evident social change.

When the container of a couple's relationship leaks and cracks in our own twenty-first-century world and one or both of the partners come to us for help, how can we best conceptualize their pain and intervene effectively using psychoanalytic principles? This is the central theme of Dr. Thomas's chapter. I turn my attention now to her two case examples, first that of Paul and his wife Irene, then that of the Quinns.

Intriguingly, Dr. Thomas includes in her "stories from the edge" of couples in distress not only a couple but also an individual, Paul, whose wife, Irene, she has never met. Dr. Thomas tells us that she has "always had in mind that Paul is part of a couple," so much so that "even if Paul had never mentioned his wife, I would have had a notion of her." I wonder why Dr. Thomas experiences Paul in this way, especially since it was not trouble in his marriage that brought Paul to therapy, but rather the long-term, profound effects of a chaotic, violent upbringing as the only child of alcoholic parents. The gains Paul has made in therapy have allowed this middle-aged man to deal with the practical daily problems of living—such as a broken cistern, or a dead car battery—with more flexibility and less panic and paranoia. We can presume that as he has tamed his harsh superego, and freed himself of its roots in a punishing religious faith and an abusive mother, Paul has taken in Dr. Thomas as a good parent, a forgiving and loving figure who, as Hans Loewald would tell us, can recognize him as something more than he is at present (Loewald, 2000, p. 243).

And yet, there is the matter of Paul's marriage to Irene, not on the edge of divorce, but rather lacking any edge at all, in Dr. Thomas's estimation. Their marriage container has failed like their broken cistern, and while their battery has been recharged and then replaced, we anticipate it will die again before too long. Irene, it seems, has limited social and perhaps cognitive capabilities, and she cannot bond with Paul in a mature sexual relationship. Paul's newly developed integration and self-esteem perhaps have left Irene far behind, but, as he tells Dr. Thomas, he accepts the situation and has hope that Irene might change over time, as has he. In this hope, Dr. Thomas sees further evidence of Paul's capacity to love, to trust, and to commit himself to the future of his relationship with Irene, despite its frustrating lack of intimacy.

Is it perhaps this longing for intimacy, both emotional and physical, that makes Dr. Thomas so aware of Paul as part of a couple? She speculates on his possible transference to her as the small, brusque woman in the back of the shop, who not only finds but also installs the right part in the car and gets it going again. This installation makes possible Paul and Irene's reconnection, but I wonder too about the erotic charge in the consulting room, which might clue Dr. Thomas in to Paul's sexuality and to the existence of his female partner. Perhaps Paul's experience of his therapist as an object of desire, and her own awareness of him as a man, enable the new sexual assertiveness he demonstrates in the lake with Irene, and his confidence that eventually his wife might turn around.

The story of Paul and Irene, in my view, evocatively portrays aspects of Dr. Thomas's rural homeplace. There are plenty of troubles, and life is hard. No one expects an easy time of it. When problems mount up, people some-times break down. But in the end what matters most is having someone's back, them having yours, and the capacity to love and work. Dr. Thomas's story beautifully depicts a psychoanalytic therapist helping her adult patient get back on track after a soul-crushing childhood. Starting from a position of despair and hopelessness, she works with him to explore a dark past, make a new attachment to her, and—again thinking of Loewald, as explicated by Jonathan Lear—accept responsibility for his own needs and wishes, rather than holding himself responsible (Lear, 2000, p. xxxvi).

From this more integrated position Paul can hope that marriage to Irene might get better, while also accepting her very serious limitations as an intimate partner. Dr. Thomas hasn't treated them as a couple, but by helping Paul feel he can effectively get the cistern rebuilt, she also helps him imagine his lifeless marriage as a container worth repairing. He has an idea of what a mature marital triangle might be. Hope, a major theme in Dr. Thomas's chapter, has found root in Paul.

I would like to consider again why any of us, like Dr. Thomas, might feel we have an idea of an individual's partner even if they have never been mentioned or described in therapy. I have already speculated on the erotic transference/countertransference connection that might run between Paul and Dr. Thomas, and the vision she holds in her mind of his future growth. But there is more, for Dr. Thomas tells us: "I do not understand Paul and Irene to represent a 'creative couple.' ... However, I do think that Paul brings to the marriage many of the qualities that contribute to a mature couple relationship, such as an appreciation for the relationship itself as a vital component, a sense of both autonomy and dependency, relinquishment of grandiosity, and acceptance of reality." Perhaps Paul brings these positions both to the marriage, and to the work he does with his therapist, so she can well imagine him in relation to a partner.

The capacity for hope might be a component of what Paul brings to therapy, or thinking from within other theoretical frameworks, qualities such as resilience or grit. Most of all, I believe Dr. Thomas refers here to commitment to repairing the container, however long that may take, and in the meantime, resolving to bring water in from elsewhere. She doesn't tell us about all it has taken over years of therapeutic work for Paul to recover from the brink of collapse and to have the fortitude to choose estrangement from his toxic mother, but we might surmise that Dr. Thomas has always understood loyalty and the ability to stay close to another person as among Paul's strengths.

Dr. Thomas's story of Paul makes me think about the converse experience I have had with some people in treatment who may talk about the same partner for years but never quite make me feel that I have a strong sense of them as part of a couple, or of that other person in their lives. In some cases, they are stuck in a stale, pale relationship that no longer works but feel unable to leave because of too many past losses or too much guilt; the thought of separation brings up intolerable anxiety. In others, though, following Dr. Thomas's formulation, what is lacking is the ability to imagine oneself as part of a third, and to take a depressive rather than a paranoid position when disruption invariably occurs. Thus, I only wind up hearing about two separate individuals, rather than a matching, or even mismatched, pair. Those who have lacked sufficient containment in their childhood—sometimes themselves children of divorced parents—may experience great difficulty when attempting to construct an adult container with someone else.

This observation brings me to Dr. Thomas's two-part story of a couple on the verge of uncoupling, the Quinns. I note that Dr. Thomas has given names in very different registers to the patients in her chapter. Paul and Irene get harmonious first names, neither too common nor uncommon, that may inspire all sorts of associations. Mr. and Mrs. Quinn have only a last name, starting with an odd letter, a big question mark perhaps. Does the intimacy of the name correspond to the depth of the work in each case? Or does it have to do with the level of hope each conveys?

As I remarked earlier, the thread of hope as a counterpoint to the threat of divorce, a thread either tightly woven into the fabric of a marriage or frayed nearly beyond repair, runs as a constant through both of Dr. Thomas's stories. Paul's hope may be enough to keep him and Irene together in their flawed marriage, from which neither apparently wants to separate; it is a story of sustained hope in the face of unremitting disaster. For the Quinns, the hope of a future together first dissipates, then reappears, at opposite ends of the spectrum. The two parts of their story offer positive and negative portraits of what couple therapy can and cannot accomplish, therapy terminable and interminable, hope and hopelessness. With these two vignettes we are given the worst and best case scenarios of psychoanalytically informed couple therapy.

Dr. Thomas summarizes several important contributions to the literature theorizing the couple relationship from a psychoanalytic perspective, and I have alluded to two already: the containing function of marriage and the marital triangle. Both imply that to work as a well-running pair, a couple must create an entity—whether we call it the marriage, or the committed couple relationship—larger than its individual components, a third greater than the sum of its two parts. Dr. Thomas explicates these theories and their origins in analytic thinking about the dyad and the Oedipal triangle quite succinctly as she tells the stories of her work with Paul and with the Quinns. She also meditates on the usefulness or limits of her own role as therapist facing a couple now edging toward a split, and especially on her own countertransference in each case.

The Quinns, part I, cause Dr. Thomas to feel bored, impotent, helpless, and finally invisible and ignored. I confess that as I read about her difficult work with this couple, I found myself wondering where there was any space for hope, other than a divorce that might be less than savage—though even that seemed a remote possibility. If we think about a couple's relationship developmentally, as an entity progressing or regressing through different stages over time, getting off track, then on again, the Quinns seem not only uncoupled and disconnected but quite hopelessly derailed and wrecked. Mrs. Quinn's investment in cherishing rage and making her husband pay for his infidelity overshadows everything else good that might transpire; these sessions have been set up by her not to repair the container but to bring Mr. Quinn down with her into profound depths of betrayal and despair. Dr. Thomas quite effectively conveys what it is like for a therapist to enter this sadomasochistic dynamic, which, as she tells us, is sad but not uncommon, and she ends her initial story of the Quinns with several questions about where to go from here, all based in taking some form of action—medication, sex therapy, homework.

To me, this bleak conclusion signals that hope might only come in the form of someone or something in addition to the container Dr. Thomas offers in psychoanalytically informed therapy. Like a severely disturbed individual, it seems it would take a team, or a village, to repair this couple's broken trust and love. A village, perhaps, like the one of Dr. Thomas's childhood, where social support might counter the vicious cycle of narcissistic rage in which both Quinns are mired. We don't know much about the Quinns as people connected to a larger world through children, work, or extended family, and so their story inspires, at least for me, yet more questions with no answers.

Are they a couple in their forties despairing as they enter middle age? Parents whose children no longer hold them together? An immigrant couple who have been challenged to mourn and adapt, and failed (Grinberg and Grinberg, 1989; Akhtar, 2011)? Or deeply traumatized people both in need of individual, as well as couples therapy?

Graciela Abelin-Sas and Peter Mezan (2009), clinicians engaged in collaborative research on the psychoanalysis of couples, refer to the "synergizing potential of individual and couple treatments." Abelin-Sas (2011) writes, "From a transference perspective, my position changes constantly in relation with each member of the couple … I tend to think that the most archaic transferences towards me are better elucidated in their individual therapies." She continues, "The presence of a third person is an important parameter in itself. We are speaking of an active third person: active in the very fact of her gestures and questions, her personal interest and emotional involvement. In this sense we cannot speak of analytic neutrality but rather a visible, real person. The therapist does not establish alliances with individuals but with the couple itself; in this way she reaffirms that they are one entity."

Dr. Thomas at first cannot be this kind of active therapist with the Quinns, who fill the space with their individual pain and talk over her; instead, she feels invisible, and retreats in the face of attacks made by Mrs. Quinn in particular. In contrast, in part II of their story, she is able to serve as an active, engaged third person, feeling more at ease and able "to look more carefully at the couple before me." Dr. Thomas can do this because the Quinns have begun to laugh together rather than at each other, feeling less pressure to demand answers and partisan support from their therapist. They have apparently repaired the failing container of their marriage enough to work in therapy as a pair, as two points of a newly intact marital triangle. Just how this shift occurs is left a mystery by Dr. Thomas, so we don't know how she understands the change or what has most been most effective in achieving it. Somehow there is now a less precipitous edge, less urgency, and Dr. Thomas has more time in session to adjust her perspective while looking at the couple, to see and feel what lies beyond the edge of their manifest difficulties.

It is in the context of this greatly improved relationship that Mrs. Quinn's health crisis emerges. Now we see the Quinns acting in the larger social world I wondered about earlier, mobilizing doctors, family, and friends to aid them as they face the diagnosis and treatment of a serious illness. Will the marriage serve as a container through this process, or break apart under added stress? Dr. Thomas describes a session in which old patterns of destructive conflict between the couple threaten to recur, taking away hope and solidarity at a critical time.

Interestingly, the conflict arises when Mrs. Quinn creates a triangle extending beyond the marriage by insisting that her husband talk to his visiting

mother about their situation. Mr. Quinn refuses, stating that his wife's concept of the degree of daily closeness between mother and son is exaggerated,
and that he does not confide in his mother as she imagines. In fact, he says,
he calls his mother weekly, not daily, mainly to support her in her role as
caretaker to Mr. Quinn's ailing father. He doesn't wish to burden her further
with his own troubles, from a faraway distance, when there is little she can
do to help. He prefers to reach out to local male friends, some of whom have
dealt with their own wives' illnesses, for support if he needs it. The reality
of an immigrant family separated by distance from close relatives becomes
evident in this vignette. With her in-laws visiting, Mrs. Quinn has the wishful
fantasy that geographical distance might be erased and a longed-for family
intimacy—which may never have existed in the first place—re-created.

Dr. Thomas sees Mrs. Quinn's defensive regression into an aggressive, absolute stance as a symptom of her vulnerable physical state.
Countertranferencially, the therapist holds her breath like a diver about to
go under water, perhaps feeling flooded by so much intense emotion in the
room. Dr. Thomas recognizes Mrs. Quinn's wish to take care of both her husband and herself, and her fears of not being able to cope with her diagnosis,
as the cause of her defensiveness. I would add to this conscious concern the
unconscious need, when feeling inadequate, to find her husband also coming
up short and not good enough. Instead of relying on the strength of their own
marital triangle as a source of support, she brings her mother-in-law into the
constellation, putting Mr. Quinn back into the position of a needy little boy,
not a man. Fortunately, he demonstrates a new potency by standing up to
his wife's insistence that he talk to his mother, instead asserting his right to
choose other men, his male peers, as his confidantes.

If we recall that Mrs. Quinn set up couple therapy as a punishment for Mr.
Quinn's infidelity, dragging him to see a woman therapist he didn't want to
talk to, this scene takes on even deeper meaning. "If I need to talk to someone, I want it to be someone of my own choosing," he tells his wife. She
tries to repeat the old sadomasochistic dynamic, this time by pushing him to
make himself uncomfortably vulnerable with his own mother, but he doesn't
engage her in this dance. He steers clear of the edge and manages to pull her
back as well. We might surmise that the harsh fact of her illness has forced
both of them to confront the futility of staying stuck in hurtful, defensive
conflict, and allowed them to take in the therapist as a third, now succeed-
ing in her efforts to help repair their damaged union. Dr. Thomas depicts her
experience of the more honest conversation that ensues as one of expansive
streets and roundabouts, everything moving in the right direction, a relationship back on track.

In the end, with a life-changing crisis staring them in the face, the Quinns
rediscover their joint project and commitment to each other. The therapist

accompanies them to the edge, but does not let them fall in, nor herself drown. With her steadfast intervention, they get on the road and take up the path of their life together again with regained hope. Hearing the story of the Quinns, part II, we believe their battery, their repaired container, has the juice and the potential to last a while.

Dr. Thomas's chapter concludes with remarks on several broad concepts. She first makes an analogy between the art of a psychoanalyst working with unconscious processes and that of an artist drawing the negative space around an object, rather than the object itself, using a conscious and intended shift of perspective. Dr. Thomas's work with the Quinns, I believe, illustrates how the analyst working with a couple in severe distress often has little chance in session to take up that broader perspective in an intentional way. Couples may not come in to consult with us until one of the partners has already (perhaps silently) decided they want to end the relationship, and the edges of conflict are about to separate into an irreparable chasm. The analyst, as Dr. Thomas has shown, must rely on her own countertransference to understand what lies beyond the edge. At the same time, a more active therapist able to engage the couple as a unit as well as two separate individuals may help them achieve mature relational qualities that will preclude further destruction, no matter what the outcome. The Quinns ultimately were able to use the help they obtained from Dr. Thomas—and her own consultant—to stay together, but the story could have also ended in divorce, amiable or less so.

Dr. Thomas understands the process of achieving such mature relational capacity as one of redemption. I am intrigued by this use of a concept both theological and transactional in a psychoanalytic context. The possible redemption of a troubled relationship in the theological sense, of course, is what "marriage counseling," often offered by clergy, used to mean. "Can this marriage be saved?" asks the popular, long-running column of the *Ladies' Home Journal*, in existence even today. Dr. Thomas asserts that the psychoanalytic tasks of promoting more flexible and fluid emotional functioning, the development of a capacity to tolerate ambivalent feelings, and the acceptance of loss and mourning as an inevitable part of human experience result in such a redemption. The person or couple who achieve this level of maturity is brought "out of human pain and suffering and into the light of acceptance and presence." Presumably, the attainment of a higher self or selves, with good outweighing evil, saves both the couple and all those around them from the anguish of further destructive conflict.

If we think of the other definition of redemption, the commercial and transactional one of purchasing back something already sold or repaying a debt, we might also consider what happens to legacies of intergenerational trauma in a psychoanalytic treatment. Dr. Thomas's work with Paul amply shows how a person exposed to multiple traumas in childhood may repeat that suffering until damaging internal objects are replaced by the more benign presence of a caring therapist. In a similar way, Mr. and Mrs. Quinn bring unconscious transferences born of traumatic separation to their relationship, repeating again and again the pain of betrayal and loss with their therapist as witness, until they can finally move forward together. Redemption in this sense would mean regaining the better life that had previously been taken away, and the interruption of traumatic repetition through a new and healing experience in analytic therapy.

I will conclude with the concept of metaphor, a trope running through both Dr. Thomas's chapter and my own. Dr. Thomas identifies metaphor as the vehicle we use to convey a psychoanalytic understanding of unconscious processes and profound human experience that elude more prosaic language. Metaphor, then, represents the poetry of psychoanalysis.

My epigraph, fittingly, is taken from the 1992 Nobel Lecture of Caribbean poet Derek Walcott. There he speaks of the islands of the Antilles as fragments comprising the epic memory of African, Asian, and European cultures, as well as a violent history of colonialism, slavery, and servitude. Those fragments and their constantly changing landscape create something beautiful out of that traumatic history. Although the pain is never forgotten by their inhabitants, daily life moves forward with dignity and resolve. Describing his beloved Antilles, Walcott offers the metaphor of a broken and re-glued vase, reassembled with a love stronger than the love that took for granted its former wholeness in Africa and Asia. So too might we understand the love uniting fragments of a containing relationship that has withstood rupture and repair to be strengthened by its scars and edges, metaphors for profound psychic change.

Chapter Eight

The Intersection of Divorce, Psychoanalytic Theory, and Clinical Practice

A Concluding Commentary

Suzanne Benser

Growth results from ruptures that have been repaired. Separation from the breast, separation and individuation from the primary object, and the oedipal complex invariably bring rupture of earlier self and relational experiences. Throughout the life cycle, our trajectory is a series of intrapsychic and interpersonal experiences of loss that can lead to increasing mastery and mentalization, object relatedness, and intersubjectivity. As developmental psychoanalytic thinkers have shown, ruptures lead to developmental growth when early attachment facilitates mourning and acceptance of what has been lost.

The Margaret Mahler symposium this year was about the loss of Eden rediscovered: the rupture of the adult relationship that is intended to banish isolation forevermore through lifelong union and intimacy. Despite the frequency of divorce, wedding vows are still invoked with a conviction in their transformative ability to protect couples from aloneness. The contributions from this year's Mahler symposium allowed us to consider divorce from a multitude of psychoanalytic viewpoints: relational trauma and sequelae in divorcing families, developmental antecedents that contribute to difficulties with commitment and resiliency after divorce, cultural trends, and, most notably, ways of working therapeutically with patients struggling with disrupted marital relationships and separations.

MARTIN SILVERMAN'S CONTRIBUTION

In the symposium's first contribution, "Divorce Is Not Good for Children and Other Living Things," Martin Silverman focuses on the impact of divorce on children's development. As a child psychoanalyst, Dr. Silverman's concern for the vulnerable child is apparent throughout the chapter with evocative descriptions of the fury and defeat of children who are traumatized as the "civilian casualties" of contentious divorce. Empathy for his child patients is paired with a call to divorcing parents: "Divorce is not good for children." He expands his perspective later in the chapter to consider the effects of divorce throughout the lifespan and even across generations, as signaled in the title: "and other living things." A parallel seems be drawn between the dangers of nuclear war and the fission-like effects of divorce, with the fall out of radiation having immediate effects on families and the mutagenic effects occurring at some future time, perhaps even in future generations.

Dr. Silverman presents his view of the developmental effects of high-conflict divorce succinctly: "What happens early in life tends to influence development from that point onward and to be carried forward into adulthood, when it can reappear after having lain dormant, in the form of disturbance of various aspects of functioning or repetition (at times in disguised form) of what had been experienced in the distant past."

He provides several moving vignettes that demonstrate the immediate impact of highly contentious divorce on children like Billy, a ten-year-old boy who developed disrupting aggressive behaviors toward his mother and siblings, and in school. After settling into treatment with Dr. Silverman, they were able to understand that Billy was displacing his anger onto others: "it became clear that he needed his father much too much and was far too enraged at him for leaving for Billy to be able to admit to himself how hurt he felt by his father abandoning him, his mother, and his sister to become part of a different family." In another vignette, we hear the desire of a four-year-old boy in treatment to destroy his hated, divorcing parents who were using him as a weapon in their contentious divorce through the boy's fantasy of becoming invulnerable as an adult and able to retaliate: "Someday, I'm going to grow up—and then I'm going to change my name to neither of their names!" In these vignettes, Dr. Silverman shows his ability to work with the pathologic adaptations these children have made to traumatic external events, and the attendant interdigitation with instinctual drives.

With the urgency of witnessing trauma occurring to children in high-conflict divorce settings, and his developmental perspective that what happens early in life is singularly impactful, Dr. Silverman calls to parents to find ways of protecting their children. His implied hope is that calling divorcing parents' attention to how their children may be negatively affected will increase awareness and perhaps elicit guilt and remorse and lead parents to change the traumatizing behaviors. He provides excellent references for divorcing parents who may be open to focusing more on helping their children through the experience, and concludes his chaper with "I strongly recommend these books to parents who are ending or have ended their marriage, as well as to those in the mental health and legal professions who work with them."

Dr. Silverman moves on to share two excellent clinical vignettes in which the lifelong impact of divorce in adult patients is well demonstrated. In the first of these vignettes, Diane, a married woman in her thirties with multiple difficulties, was able to work effectively with Dr. Silverman: "She gradually realized, however, that far more important was her rage at her mother for depriving her of a relationship with the father whom she never had ceased idealizing and who, unconsciously, she never had ceased hoping would return to her. She remembered that her mother, when she was angry at her, periodically blamed her for the breakup of the marriage—because her father had not wanted a child at that time. It took a great deal of work to help Diane sort all of this all and disentangle the past from the present."

The last vignette is of Eddie, a married man who had recently become a father. Eddie had been unable to form trusting relationships and sought out treatment "because he was engaging compulsively in activities that threatened the stability of his marriage." Dr. Silverman takes us back to see Eddie as a victim of relational trauma as a child, and then to the present and probable future as a husband and father likely to abandon both his wife and newborn child. "Even with his little daughter, who was just a few months old, he was frightened because he 'did not feel an all-encompassing, unbreakable love for her.' It also troubled him that he felt hurt and angry at her whenever she cried, didn't respond to him when he wanted her to, or leaned toward her mommy instead of toward him to soothe and comfort her." Dr. Silverman conveys his ability to accept and understand Eddie's difficulties with attachment as the downstream effect of the fracturing of his family unit and unprocessed early abandonment that in turn led him not to risk attachment with his daughter and wife, and to his inability to continue in treatment.

This depiction of Eddie conceptualizes relational trauma due to divorce as not only leading to downstream effects in an individual's life but also leading to difficulties in parenting and thus an intergenerational transmission of trauma. The inclusion of the following study also supports that conceptualization: "Daniel Offer and Melvin Sabshin (1966), in an important, normative study of adolescence, found that the group that sailed through adolescence swimmingly was the one that contained teenagers with families that not only were intact but had been solidly secure for several generations."

Dr. Silverman moves from that developmental conceptualization to a more judgmental view of divorcing parents in other areas of the chapter, as in this quote that implies divorcing parents are simply unwilling or inadequate to care for their children, "parents show themselves to be incapable of uniting together to handle life's challenges and of ironing out the inevitable wrinkles that develop in a relationship between two people," and "not all parents,

furthermore, are equally capable of freeing themselves from being preoccupied with their own narcissistic injury and narcissistic rage over what is
taking place to tune in and respond helpfully to what their children are experiencing." This judgmental view of parents could even be seen as shifting
parents into the position of willful perpetrators: "One of the most devastating
scenarios, in my experience, is the one in which parental divorce leads to loss
of a parent, either because of abandonment or because one parent, usually the
mother, demonizes the other parent and blocks him from having access to the
children." In another description of divorce, Dr. Silverman clearly evokes a
willfully destructive female: "I am inclined to say that divorces are like that
little girl in the nursery rhyme who had a little curl in the middle of her forehead. When they are good, they are very, very good—and when they are bad,
they are horrid!" In these descriptions, I imagine Dr. Silverman conveying
the child's urgent appeals of "See what they are doing to me!" and "See how
horrible they are!" to an authority figure.

Witnessing parents traumatize children must illicit feelings of urgency
in any compassionate bystander. That urgency when working with children
in psychotherapy could only be compounded by the awareness that both
under-responding and over-responding to a traumatized child could be re-
traumatizing (Balint, 1969). Intervening effectively in cycles of abuse has
proven to be a challenge of worldwide proportions with few answers, but
with most experts agreeing that validating a history of trauma is necessary for
victims who are perpetrating the cycle in order for them to make reparations
(Goldner, 2004). A call to parents in high-conflict divorce might be more
clearly received by asserting the possibility of trauma playing a role in the
involvement of their children and moving away from the identification with
the wronged child to a perspective in which the unprocessed trauma is consistently seen in the struggling parent, as Dr. Silverman does so expertly in
the clinical vignettes with adult patients. He is accepting of his adult patients'
flaws and destructive behaviors as manifestations of earlier relational trauma,
and as aspects of their personalities that are understandable and attenuated
through psychotherapy. It seems likely that his patient Diane has become
more satisfied in her marriage and more available as a mother as a result of
the work she did with Dr. Silverman. A life-affirming view of the benefits of
intensive psychotherapy in repairing and processing trauma with a caring and
respectful psychoanalyst is a call that a struggling parent seems more likely
to heed.

Accepting and identifying with the vulnerability of divorcing parents
would also mean relinquishing a fantasy of an all-powerful self-object that
could admonish the neglected child's parents into heeding culture's dictum to
sacrifice for one's children, and could reanimate the child's zombie objects.
Jessica Benjamin eloquently describes the difficulty in giving up this fantasy:

"But why should mothers, or anyone, be able to guarantee this safety to children in a life in which we are all subject to a variety of slings and arrows? We suspect that the heightened expectations of provision may enter our minds more by channeling our baby selves, baby fears and desires (e.g., unconscious fears of environmental failure, annihilation, abandonment), than merely by dint of social inflation and competition. Yet the confusion of good enough mothering with the ability to protect children and give them a perfect life ('his majesty the baby' [Freud, 1914]) seems indeed a cultural discourse, an artifact of what Lasch (1979) dubbed the culture of narcissism. The direction of effects is doubled: discourses into which we are interpellated have, as psychoanalysts insist, origins in specific infantile or childhood fantasies" (Benjamin, 2011).

Just as the antinuclear slogan "War is not good for children and other living things" heralded the demise of an earlier American worldview in which a strong military brought us invisibility, the warning that divorce is "not good for children and other living things" may allude to the waning in the twenty-first century of our collective nuclear family ideal in which paternalistic and heterosexist normative forces have not been able to overcome the radioactive effects of narcissism and sadomasochism on relationships. For children in families experiencing high-conflict divorce at this moment in history in which the family ideal is in the midst of transformation and the culture of narcissism is still pervasive, the idealization of an aspirational family cannot repair cycles of traumatic ruptures across generations without the containment of an empathically attuned, trusting relationship that can hold all the interwoven vulnerable, loving, and destructive aspects of humanity.

JOSHUA EHRLICH'S CONTRIBUTION

Joshua Ehrlich's contribution, "Some Countertransference Challenges in Working with Divorcing Adults," invites us to join him in understanding the divorcing adult patient and some characteristic ways the divorce setting can impact the therapeutic relationship. He opens the chapter with his theoretical premise that can be summarized as follow: Divorce is inevitably experienced as a loss, and the individual's experience of earlier developmental losses becomes entwined in the current presentation. He extends the premise by noting that difficulties with earlier losses can lead to difficulties in mourning the loss of the marriage, which results in clinical presentations that are often misleading. This is a developmental perspective in which he defines mourning quite broadly, combining the concepts of Klein's states of mind as oscillating between the paranoid/schizoid and depressive positions and Freud's (1917b) conceptualization that melancholia signals unresolved mourning. Dr. Ehrlich

then uses explanations of ego psychological defense mechanisms, object relations theory, and countertransference theories as a primer for understanding
potentially misleading clinical presentations in the divorcing patient.

Dr. Ehrlich follows with two case vignettes in which each of the patients
presents with minimal signs of loss or mourning. In the first vignette, Dr.
Ehrlich and Mr. A. join in constructing a divorce narrative in which Mr. A.
is pleased to be leaving a marriage that has "lacked intimacy for years."
The ex-wife is cast as "brittle, unpleasant and retaliatory," justifying Mr.
A.'s affair with a more pleasing woman. After a few months, Dr. Ehrlich
steps away from the identification with his patient and, oriented with a
developmental perspective, conceptualizes Mr. A.'s lack of conscious
experience of loss as a disavowal and projection of split-off bad self parts
onto the ex-wife due to intolerance of mourning in the depressive position. Dr. Ehrlich says to Mr. A.: "'I find it a bit hard to believe that the
marriage was as awful as you describe. Can you tell me about some close
times with your wife?' Mr. A. sat quietly for a few minutes, pondered and
then began to cry. He sat weeping for several minutes. When he was able
to talk, he expressed shock that he was so sad because he had no idea he
felt that way." Mr. A. experienced sadness following this interpretation,
indicating that his initial presentation was likely a regression from the
depressive position to the paranoid schizoid position with development
enabled through mourning in therapy.

In the second vignette, we hear a similar conceptualization with Ms. B.
unable to mourn the loss of her marriage ideal and a regression to the paranoid
schizoid position: "Ms. B. alternated between a focus on her husband's positive features—his intelligence, business successes, lively personality—and her
sinking feeling that she had been taken in by him. She had found credit card
receipts that indicated he was spending up to $1,000/month on strip clubs and
she also found evidence of cocaine use. At first, she denied what she saw and
assumed she was exaggerating her concerns." Ms. B.'s presentation seemed to
be a projection of idealized all good self and object parts onto the husband, in
contrast with Mr. A.'s presenting view of his ex-wife as all-bad.

In both cases, Dr. Ehrlich describes overidentification with each patient
early in the treatment. With Mr. A. he writes: "For my own personal reasons,
it was easier for me initially to take some pleasure in his harsh, dismissive
portrait of his wife than to open myself up to the tragedy in the situation; however, that reverberated in my own psyche. Mr. A., unconsciously, pressured
me to buttress his defensive distancing from his loving feelings (and the sorrow that attached to them)." With Ms. B., he describes his internal state: "In
identification with her, I became fuzzy in my thinking for a time, wondering
if I, too, was exaggerating the severity of the problem and then, alternately,

recognizing just how bad things had become. In retrospect, I think that I also became a participant in the reenactment of a family drama: I was the mother who, for her own defensive needs, was unable to help her daughter process harsh reality." The overidentifications in both cases were ruptured when Dr. Ehlrich turned to his private, inner state and then shared interpretations formulated from his reverie: "As I recognized my defensive denial, I began to confront Ms. B. with hers. Over the course of several months, Ms. B. began to acknowledge more fully that her husband was out of control and her marriage was untenable." Dr. Ehrlich conceptualized Mr. A. and Ms. B. as patients who were able to move out of their regressed positions and mourn the loss of marriage with help in tolerating ambivalence and increasing integration of love and hate. Dr. Ehrlich implies that the experience of his patients being understood by him in psychotherapy may have served to repair the ruptured identifications and facilitate mourning as well, evoking the therapeutic aspects as a new object relationship.

Dr. Ehrlich moves away from exploring the dynamics of his patients within the therapeutic relationship to a broader perspective in the second half of his chapter when he specifically addresses the second topic: technical challenges in working with divorcing adults. His stance is more removed when describing a clinical vignette with Mr. C. and Ms. D., and he focuses primarily on the mental health and legal professionals involved in their case. He states, "Working with people in acrimonious divorces is most treacherous when therapists are insufficiently aware of the force field that surrounds them." He scouts that force field for the unfamiliar therapist by introducing pertinent theories and citing a range of experts in divorce giving the reader an overview of high-conflict divorces. Dr. Ehrlich notes, "Not surprisingly many people who lock into bitter, ongoing acrimony suffered early losses or massive narcissistic traumas. According to Jan Johnston, the foremost writer and researcher on high-conflict divorce (who also integrates psychodynamic ideas into her writing), about two thirds of people in high-conflict divorces have Axis II diagnoses, including paranoid, borderline and schizoid personality disorders."

Dr. Ehrlich's technical advice to therapists working with patients in the high-conflict divorce setting is to maintain a neutral stance with attention to any pulls to action and to seek the presence of a third influence external to the dyad by openly addressing ethical considerations and making use of consultation or outside resources. He describes the risks of overidentification paired with acting out in the portrayal of Mr. C.'s local psychiatrist who did not maintain a third perspective. Dr. Ehrlich also recognizes the difficulty in maintaining empathy for divorcing patients in other situations, for example, when "parents in high-conflict divorces tend to do awful things to their children—like maligning their other parent or interfering with the parent's access to the child—and feel entirely justified in doing so."

Expanding the developmental "primer" in the chapter could have added depth to the understanding of the "force field that surrounds" therapists when working with these patients and have allowed Jan Johnston's research to be more clinically applicable. Peter Fonagy's views on mentalization, trauma, and personality disorders are particularly germane: "There is a mutual developmental relationship between trauma and mentalising; trauma may undermine the child's willingness to play with feelings and ideas (felt as too real) in relation to external events, but at the same time, the lack of a full mentalising mode of internal organisation will create a propensity for the continuous repetition of the trauma, in the absence of the modulation which a representational view of psychic reality brings" (Fonagy and Target, 2000).

Dr. Ehrlich notes, "Though high-conflict divorces are more volatile and inflammatory than more ordinary divorces, their dynamics are essentially the same—two people struggling emotionally to disengage from a (presumably) close relationship and employing defenses to deal with painful affects." The use of the word *presumably* in parenthesis perhaps speaks to the possibility that not all patients are defending against feelings of loss of closeness, or hoped for closeness, when divorcing. Stanley Ruszcynski, as coeditor of the book *Intrusiveness and Intimacy in the Couple*, writes, "Sometimes apparent intimacy is an expression of an intrusive determination to control the other. At heart such intrusiveness consists in treating the other as an extension of the self ... an 'intimacy' of projective identification, an intimacy that is delusional as it denies separateness" (Ruszczynski, 1995). Thus, the end of a marriage for a person like Mr. C., who manipulates others, may not be associated with intolerable sadness, but rather experienced as a threat to the sense of self. The defenses employed by Mr. C. may have been enacting dissociated self-states in "pretend mode" in which he is "able to say anything and try to do anything to the relationship without any consequences for outer reality or for his or her frame of mind" (Fonagy and Target, 2004) to feel he is "going on being" and defend against annihilation fears (Winnicott, 1956).

A patient in the high-conflict divorce setting who has not developed mentalization capacities will also not relate to the therapist as a separate, potentially valued partner in understanding their own experiences. Ehrlich ends his chapter with advice to therapists to reach out for consultation and outside resources to intervene in escalating traumatic separations. This advice seems to be both for the benefit of families going through a high-conflict divorce and for the benefit of the therapist. The experience of being used by a patient as if the therapist were an actor in a play that the patient directs can undermine the therapist's confidence in the power of the therapeutic alliance.

ELIZABETH THOMAS'S CONTRIBUTION

Elizabeth Thomas does take us to those moments of hopelessness in the therapist, and then brings us back from the edge with the promise of possible redemption. In her evocative chapter "Stories from the Edge: Divorce as Redemption," Dr. Thomas shares a subjective experience of futility in working psychoanalytically with the Quinns, a couple in treatment who are embroiled in a sadomasochist war.

Before focusing on that experience, Dr. Thomas begins the chapter with a wide-angle view that pans the normative landscape of marriage and divorce. She is in a postmodern, post-apocalyptic mode, having lived through divorce herself. We hear her assessment of the landscape outside of Eden where now "marriage is less the norm than in years past," and where we are many years away from her childhood home in rural Virginia when she never knew anyone who was divorced. The allusion to divorce as redemption in the title portends the journey her chapter takes us on, where there can be no return to Eden, but redemption perhaps found through connections that allow acceptance of our fallen, flawed selves.

In contrast with Dr. Silverman's locus of intervention on the child and Dr. Ehrlich's on the individual, Dr. Thomas puts forth that "troubled couple relationships are the precursor to separation and divorce. Intervention is needed at the point of the couple in distress because help at this point can improve the well-being of the adults themselves and establish a firm base for children. Intervention at the couple level serves to strengthen individuals and families, and to provide healthful transitions in the event of ultimate separation." To that end she orients us to her theoretical perspective in which Kleinian, Neo-Klenian, and relational writers inform her understanding of an individual's development and the dynamics at play when working with a couple in psychoanalytic treatment: "So these theoretical concepts begin to come together: containment, thirds and triangles, capacity, and ultimately something beyond the obvious that has to be created within relationship. These ideas, drawn from psychoanalytic work with individuals, are efforts to conceptualize the complex, multilayered, and often furiously paced world of relationship. It is to these ideas that the therapist can appeal for some notion of how and to what end the therapeutic work can bend."

Dr. Thomas then moves to a clinical example in which "intervention at the couple level serves to strengthen individuals and families" with the vignette of the Quinns, a couple in crisis following the discovery of Mr. Quinn's infidelity. Through descriptions of their interactions, Dr. Thomas demonstrates powerful cycles of projected and introjected paranoid/schizoid destructive fears and fantasies. "Mr. Quinn goes on, making banal advances—'I'm trying to connect with you'; Mrs. Quinn, averting her eyes, is spiteful— 'you spoil it, always.'"

"Mrs. Quinn swipes away his overtures like so many crumbs" and "Mr. Quinn makes an effort—several, in fact. He selects a very nice café for lunch and he shows interest in Mrs. Quinn's opinion of the food. He seems to want to connect. He makes a bid, but Mrs. Quinn turns away." Mr. Quinn's fear that his aggression/betrayal has destroyed the object relationship is projected onto Mrs. Quinn with his repeated contrite overtures. Mrs. Quinn in turn responds with introjection/identification and repudiation of the injured, vulnerable, needy object. Mrs. Quinn cannot tolerate this vulnerable position, even with its attendant potential for comfort, and instead invokes righteous indignation casting Mr. Quinn as the damaged, flawed one. Dr. Thomas also feels rebuffed in her efforts to intercede in the couple's sadomasochistic lockstep and looks for a psychoanalytic understanding of the sadomasochistic rejection of repair of the rupture. She conceptualizes the difficulties as impaired mentalization, with Mrs. Quinn choosing rejection of reparation as less dangerous to the pathologic defense of her sense of self as incompetent. She appealed to Dr. Thomas to witness the betrayal, to join her in rejecting her husband: "She had claimed, loudly, that I was too easy on him, that I needed to 'call it like it is!'" Dr. Thomas's psychoanalytic understanding helped her resist being pulled into Mrs. Quinn's urgency or to perhaps "call it like it is" from the perspective of seeing Mrs. Quinn as the injuring one who would not accept the efforts of repair that both Mr. Quinn and Dr. Thomas offered. Despite her assessment that the couple was profoundly disconnected, and that the therapy was a farce in which she was used as a tool to enact both of the individuals' narcissistic needs, Dr. Thomas remained open to waiting and asked the reader to join her in waiting until later in the chapter to conclude the discussion of the couple's treatment.

In part II of the Quinn vignette, we hear the couple is functioning in a more connected and secure fashion, with Dr. Thomas included as a more valued ally. Indeed, the couple seems to have rallied in the face of Mrs. Quinn's recently diagnosed illness. The shift demonstrates the ability for individuals within themselves and, together as a couple, to oscillate between paranoid/schizoid and depressive positions in the context of secure containment. The shift also raises the possibility that the Quinns' original presentation not only reflected difficulties with attachment and mentalization but also may have represented an excitation of oedipal dynamics. From that perspective, we could view Mr. Quinn as having triumphantly won over someone from outside the dyad, and Mrs. Quinn showing prowess and pleasure in making Mr. Quinn repeatedly beg for her favor, and so reclaiming the victor status. Mr. Quinn in turn accepts the humiliation as punishment for his guilty, sinful triumph in an intertwining of erotic sadomasochism. Perhaps this was a culmination of a long-standing unconscious pact that now required the presence of a third party for further growth, first the mistress of Mr. Quinn and later Dr. Thomas, as stand-ins for the objects of murderous and erotic oedipal impulses (Loewald, 1977). Dr. Thomas notes examples of growth in the couple with Mrs. Quinn's appeal to Mr. Quinn's attachment with his mother as a source of support through her illness, and Mr. Quinn's ability to rebuff Mrs. Quinn ("murder" her) more verbally and directly. These changes may indicate a rebalancing of the erotic excitement as well as the attachment aspects of their sadomasochistic dance in which the danger and safety of familiar attachments and internalized object representations were reconfigured in a more stabilized fashion in which each partner can rebuff the other and be taken back. This development was called becoming a "creative couple" by Dr. Thomas, and it could also be thought of as a move to the postoedipal phase as described by contemporary psychoanalytic thinkers, including Jodi Davies: "From the postoedipal developmental process comes the capacity to tolerate imperfections in our love objects, to experience disappointment without the death of desire, to apprehend that true intimacy requires mutual vulnerability and psychic interpenetration" (Davies, 2003).

In a second clinical vignette, Dr. Thomas describes the way in which individual psychotherapy with a married patient can strengthen the couple's relationship. She writes, "When bad things happen, Paul typically reacts with fear, anxious that he is somehow responsible," and describes how this pathologic constellation was constructed to defend the patient against the psychic impact of an extremely traumatic childhood: "He grew up an only child in an alcoholic family where violence was common. His mother often hit him, beat him, and threatened God's wrath if he misbehaved. For Paul, God was a harsh, vengeful God that ruled the universe with punishments for every conceivable misdeed, or so that was the home atmosphere. Paul strove to be good and to please God. He even became a minister in his Fundamentalist faith in an effort to appease the dual gods of mother and the Old Testament." We hear how over time Paul began to risk seeing himself as free, autonomous, and separate, and able to act on his own behalf to assess God's presence and intentions. With treatment, he continued the trajectory, trusting himself to solve problems, to ask and receive help. This process generated an increase in hopefulness that he was able to extend to his feelings about his marriage.

SYNTHESIS AND CONCLUSION

At every moment we need to know what our effective relationship is to the desire to do good, to the desire to cure.

—*The Ethics of Psychoanalysis*, Jacques Lacan, 1959–1960

Kirshner explained Lacan's statement this way: "This means that the analyst's desire, as well as the patient's, is always in play in his attempt to sustain an ethical position" (2012). The contributors to this year's symposium show us both the commonalities and variations of ways in which psychoanalytic practitioners can implement their "desire to do good, their desire to cure." All three contributors coalesce contemporary psychoanalytic understanding that pathological organizations of the mind may be constructed to defend the patient against the psychic impact of external realities and against the ravages of internal fears and phantasies with techniques aimed at understanding together with the patient the inevitable interrelationship between the internal and external aspects. Looking at their contributions as illustrations for demonstration, we can see the commonalities as well as the variations in emphasis in their stances. Dr. Silverman privileges providing opportunities for patients to express worries that are understood as conflicts of the aggressive and sexual drives exacerbated by traumatic external circumstances. Dr. Ehrlich prioritizes providing patients opportunities to mourn the loss of the idealized oedipal object with a view that aggression is a response to narcissistic injury consistent with self psychology, object relations, and intersubjective theories. Dr. Thomas privileges understanding with acceptance of the possibility of not knowing, thus allowing for increasing complexity and deeper understanding over time and aptly demonstrating "A most powerful instantiation of surrendering to the Third, to life as it really is, not as we wish it to be" (Benjamin, 2011).

The therapist's desire, or stance, invariably contains something of the therapist's particular cultural ideals as well as their theoretical assumptions. In the arena of love, and loss of love, the therapist's stance will contain his or her own expectations in these areas as developed in context of normative ideals. Collective social ideals that provide continuity and stability to a culture are underscored by rituals that celebrate coming of age, courting, dating, weddings, and anniversaries to highlight socially desirable ways of forming peer groups and families. The negation of our normative ideals is more ambiguous and less apparent: "The losses of divorce often are more inchoate and buried, and we lack such rituals for commemorating these losses" (Betz and Thorngren, 2006), making the social meaning of divorce more difficult to discern and mourn, and also more difficult to discern in the therapist's "desire to cure."

Normative social ideals, along with the more ambiguous repudiation of nonideals, are transmitted through early relational experiences and continue to influence self-identity throughout the lifespan. Virginia Goldner writes, "There is more than 20 years of feminist scholarship supporting the idea that gender is a symbolic, social, and cultural category that structures the way romantic partners experience being a couple. Issues of gender and power are woven into the fabric of intimate life, but our field has evaded them" (2004). Relational psychoanalytic writers have expanded psychoanalytic theory using social theory to describe formative relational experiences that underlie a nonintegrated sense of self in which socially prohibited identifications are foreclosed. Mourning and melancholia may proceed through identifications with lost objects (Freud, 1917b), but foreclosed, socially prohibited identifications cannot be mourned. Judith Butler and Jessica Benjamin describe these repudiated identifications as often related to homosexual longings and gender identifications: "the search for love denied that takes the form of hating what one really is, longing for what one can never have or be" (Benjamin, 2011).

Dr. Silverman and Dr. Ehrlich did not reveal social identity indicators in the cases they described with regard to race, class or minority/majority status, and none of the contributors discussed divorce considering gender and sexual identity perspectives. These omissions may reflect the majority white, heteronormal assumption that white, heterosexual status is self-evident. This assumption can lead to difficulties "because contextualizing what is 'expected' by the analyst within a 'normative' template for the analytic process can blind us to the significance of certain emergent issues in the treatment. In short, if they are 'expected,' then they are immediately less interesting; we look at them and examine them less closely" (Davies, 2003). When Dr. Thomas noted that the Quinns were immigrants to this country, the opportunity to consider a potentially different normative experience for them was opened to the reader, and we could wonder how these differences between the couple and Dr. Thomas may have played out in the treatment. Dr. Thomas expected Mr. Quinn to feel rebuffed by the refusal of his offer of love/food with the offering of pleasing food representing a submission of narcissistic gratification to the loved object, such as the meaning of chocolates given on Valentine's Day, but perhaps a man offering food to a woman in a submissive fashion may be perceived as an attack on this couples' normative gender role representations. An additional meaning of the repeated shows of rejection of Mr. Quinn's offerings in front of Dr. Thomas may been a repudiation of the privileged colonial position in which the couple placed Dr. Thomas in an unconscious pact. With that lens, Mrs. Quinn may have been displaying freedom from oppressive norms, leaving Dr. Thomas, as the privileged representative of the majority, impotent and powerless in an unconscious enactment of societal trauma. Perhaps Mr. Quinn's mistress had been similarly disempowered, perhaps also a member of the majority culture.

Dr. Thomas also reveals the social identity of the patient in her second vignette. She describes Paul as an African American man who had been physically abused as a child. We are left wondering if intergenerational transmission of trauma due to slavery and racism may have contributed to the violence in the childhood home. Considering that possibility, we can imagine Paul's mother forming identifications with white racist aggressors while beating Paul into passive submission to a wrathful, violent, racist God imago in reenactments of trauma that transmitted the mother's fear that her son would incur increased future attacks if not submissive to authority. Through relational experiences with his black wife and white therapist, Paul began to risk taking actions on his own behalf with increasing security that rejections could be weathered, while venturing to see himself as a member of the majority society with the use of the word "we" in the following quote: "You do what you can and move on. There's no big God up there sending down thunderbolts. Look, we've been to the moon. No God. To deep space." As with the Quinns, this interchange could take on a different meaning looked at from the oedipal perspective. Perhaps the reference to "no big God up there ... No God" is also an expression of a patricidal wish comingled with a wish to kill "the Man," with Dr. Thomas viewed as the oedipal mother or accomplice to the murder.

When Paul and his wife first attempted to buy a new car battery, they "had to wait in line a long time before finally getting to the clerk who, after a slow-drip trip to the back, returned to report that they did not have the battery in stock." Paul and his wife did not succumb to the defeat at the hands of the slow-drip clerk that could well have been interpreted as an instance of racism. We can envision an internalized maternal representation chastising Paul for not having been sufficiently ingratiating to the clerk and then succumbing to the paranoid position from his past. Paul does not risk protesting openly to his white therapist when bad things happen to him, but he does more effectively defend against frustration and disappointment without self-blame through profuse offerings of gratitude, and acceptance of his "lot in life" in which "you do what you can and move on." Dr. Thomas ends the vignette with "He says he is committed to his relationship with Irene. He says he will just wait and see what happens." As Paul's trust in Dr. Thomas grows, we can imagine he will risk more open expressions of his anger and power. He has allowed Dr. Thomas to see him as a virile man who wants an adult sexual relationship with his wife despite conveying the impression that the marital relationship is asexual, "It's just ho-hum, with no spark, no life." Perhaps in time as he allows himself to be increasingly viewed as powerful, black adult he will feel more secure in acknowledging his wife's strengths as well. This reciprocity could lead to Irene engaging him with more passion, while also enabling her to more openly express anger and perhaps raise a feared possibility that she, as an adult black woman, could make Paul succumb as his mother did. Through those experiences, Paul will also have to challenge the visceral message beat into him that God/white people/Dr. Thomas would attack him if he shows a desire to be respected as an equal.

Paul was not viewed as "his majesty the baby" by his parents, and it can be assumed that this impeded the usual development of healthy narcissism.

In addition to the damage to his self-esteem, the trauma of his subjugation as a black child would have foreclosed for him the majority expectation of being anointed a bearer of the kingdom's collective ideals as an adult. The extent to which he and Irene experience ongoing exclusion from majority privilege will add to a lack of trust that their family's next generation could be included by the majority as heirs of their idealized selves, despite their growth as individuals and as a couple. A lower level of social trust by this minority couple is likely to have intermingled psychological and social determinants that can be understood more fully when explored through many vantage points.

Dr. Thomas discussed some of the changes in perception and demographics in the United States and Britain with regard to marriage and divorce. The reasons for the shift away from traditional marriage and child-rearing arrangements are too complex to delineate fully and a multitude of potential vantage points are possible from which to consider the trends—political, social, economic, biologic, demographic, and advances in medicine and technology. An excerpt from a Pew Research Center paper published in 2014 frames our young adults' social context:

> Millennials now ranging in age from 18 to 33 are relatively unattached to organized politics and religion, linked by social media, burdened by debt, distrustful of people, in no rush to marry—and optimistic about the future. Just 26% of this generation is married. When they were the age that Millennials are now, 36% of Generation X, 48% of Baby Boomers and 65% of the members of the Silent Generation were married. They are also the most racially diverse generation in American history. Some 43% of Millennial adults are non-white, the highest share of any generation. Their racial diversity may partly explain Millennials' low levels of social trust.

The normative ideal of the white heterosexual American nuclear family with its privileged legal and political position has become increasingly at odds with the reality of our diverse culture and our ethics of equality and non-discrimination. Race, class, sexual, and gender identity and majority/minority status as well as marital status all have private and public aspects that join psychoanalytic theory and social theory. In therapeutic settings where the focus of treatment is on experiences with such overt social and psychological aspects, the intersection of the two aspects will be most apparent in the prioritization and processing of ethical considerations. As noted by Dr. Ehrlich at the end of his chapter, "In stepping into a high-conflict divorce, though, all of us have clinical and ethical obligations to consider the impact of our interventions on the family as a whole." Lacan's dictum to be aware at "every moment" of how we are implementing our desire to cure is an unobtainable ideal, but recognizing that our subjective view of divorce is in the context of normative family ideals could increase awareness of our desire in some moments of our work with divorcing patients. To accept the subjectivity of our moral compass as invariably affected by cultural norms could also allow for a more nuanced, co-constructed ethical compass to guide us in these settings. This symposium has opened the discourse "between what is intelligible, resignifying, and meaning-giving on one side and what is oppressive and normative on the other that we struggle to bear in mind" (Benjamin, 2011) in the challenging and vital work we do with patients affected by divorce.

References

Aarons, Z.A. (1975). The analyst's relocation: its effect on the transference. *International Journal of Psychoanalysis* 56: 303–319.

Abelin-Sas, G. (2011). El universo de la pareja. Reflexiones sobre el valor de la terapia psicoanalitica de pareja en el curso del tratamiento individual. *Aperturas psicoanaliticas 38*: http://www.aperturas.org/articulos. Retrieved April 12, 2016.

Abelin-Sas, G. and Mezan, P. (2009). The synergizing potential of individual and couples treatment. Some clinical illustration from a collaborative study. Presented at the 2009 Chicago IPA Congress.

Abraham, M. (2000). *Speaking the Unspeakable: Marital Violence against South Asian Immigrant Women in the United States*. New Brunswick, NJ: Rutgers University Press.

Ahrons, C. (2007). Family ties after divorce: long-term implications for children. *Family Process* 46: 53–65.

Ahrons, C. (2009). *We're Still Family*. New York, NY: Harper Collins.

Akhtar, S. (2011). *Immigration and Acculturation: Mourning, Adaptation, and the Next Generation*. Lanham, MD: Jason Aronson.

Amato, P.R. (2000). The consequences of divorce for adults and children. *Journal of Marriage and the Family* 62: 1269–1287.

Anderer, S.J. and Glass, D.J. (2000). A therapeutic jurisprudence and preventive law approach to family law. In: *Practicing Therapeutic Jurisprudence: Law as a Helping Profession*, eds. D. Stolle, D. Wexler and B. Winick, pp. 115–146. Durham, NC: Carolina Academic Press.

Arkowitz, H. and Lilienfeld, S.O. (2012). Is divorce bad for children? *Atlantic Magazine*, March 2012.

Balint, M. (1969). Trauma and the object relationship. *International Journal of Psychoanalysis*, 50: 429–435.

Baranowski, M.D. (1982). Grandparent-adolescent relations: Beyond the nuclear family. *Adolescence* 17: 575–584.

Balfour, A., Morgan, M., and Vincent, C., eds. (2012). *How Couple Relationships Shape our World: Clinical Practice, Research, and Policy Perspectives.* London, UK: Karnac Books.

Baruch, G. K., Biener, L., and Barrett, R. C. (1987). Women and gender in research on work and family stress. *American Psychologist* 42: 130–136.

Basescu, C. (2009). Shifting ground. *Contemporary Psychoanalysis* 45: 44–64.

Benjamin, J. (2004). Beyond doer and done-to: an intersubjective view of thirdness. *Psychoanalytic Quarterly* 78: 5–46.

_____ (2011). Facing reality together discussion: with culture in mind: the social third. *Studies in Gender and Sexuality* 12: 27–36.

Bengtson, V.L. and Robertson, J.F. (1985). *Grandparenthood.* Beverly Hills, CA: Sage.

Berman, W.H. (1988a). The relationship of ex-spouse attachment to adjustment following divorce. *Journal of Family Psychology* 1: 312–328.

_____ (1988b). The role of attachment in the post-divorce experience. *Journal of Personality and Social Psychology* 54: 496–503.

Betz, G. and Thorngren, J. (2006). Ambiguous loss and the family grieving process. *The Family Journal* 14: 359–365.

Bion, W. (1962). A theory of thinking. *International Journal of Psychoanalysis* 43: 306–310.

_____ (1963). *Elements of Psychoanalysis.* London, UK: Karnac Books.

Bolognini, S. (2011). *Secret Passages: The Theory and Technique of Interpsychic Relations*, transl. G. Atkinson. London, UK: Karnac Books.

Booth, A. and Amato, P. (1991). Divorce and psychological stress. *Journal of Health and Social Behavior* 32: 396–407.

Bowlby, J. (1973). *Attachment and Loss, Vol. 2: Separation: Anxiety, and Anger.* New York, NY: Basic Books.

_____ (1979). *The Making and Breaking of Affectional Bonds.* London, UK: Tavistock.

_____ (1980). *Attachment and Loss: Vol. 3: Loss: Sadness and Depression.* New York, NY: Basic Books.

_____ (1982). *Attachment and Loss: Vol. 1: Attachment (2nd ed).* New York, NY: Basic Books.

Breger, R. (1998). Love and the state: women, mixed marriages, and the law in Germany. In: *Cross-Cultural Marriage: Identity and Choice*, eds. R. Breger and R. Hill, pp. 129–152. Oxford, UK: Berg.

Bretherton, I., and Page, T. (2004). Shared or conflicting working models? Relationships in postdivorce families seen through the eyes of mothers and their preschool children. *Development and Psychopathology* 16: 551–575.

Bretherton, I., Ridgeway, D., and Cassidy, J. (1990). Assessing internal working models of the attachment relationships: an attachment story completion task for 3-year-olds. In: *Attachment in the Preschool Years: Theory, Research, and Interventions*, eds. M.T. Greenberg, D. Cicchetti, and M. E. Cummings, pp. 273–308. Chicago, IL: University of Chicago Press.

Britton, R. (1989). The missing link: parental sexuality in the Oedipus complex. In: *The Oedipus Complex Today: Clinical Implications*, ed. J. Steiner, pp. 83–101. London, UK: Karnac Books.

Brooks, D. (2006). Immigrants to be proud of. *The New York Times*, March 20, 2006.

Brown, P., Felton, B.J., Whiteman, V., and Manela, R. (1980). Attachment and distress following marital separation. *Journal of Divorce* 3: 303–317.

Bussell, D.A. (1995). A pilot study of African American children's cognitive and emotional reactions to parental separation. *Journal of Divorce and Remarriage* 25: 3–15.

Butler, J. (1995). Melancholy gender–refused identification. *Psychoanalytic Dialogues* 5: 165–180.

Buunk, B.P. and Mutsaers, W. (1999). The nature of the relationship between remarried individuals and former spouses and its impact on marital satisfaction. *Journal of Family Psychology* 13: 165–174.

Campbell, K.E., Marsden, P.V., and Hurlbert, J.S. (1986). Social resources and social-economic status. *Social Networks* 8: 97–117.

Cantor, D. (1982). Divorce: separation or separation-individuation? *American Journal of Psychoanalysis* 42: 307–313.

Carlin, J. (2008). No wonder Iceland has the happiest people on earth. www.theguardian.com/world/2008/may/18/iceland. Accessed March 31, 2016.

Cassidy, J. (2008). The nature of the child's ties. In: *Handbook of Attachment: Theory, Research and Clinical Applications, Second Edition*, eds. J. Cassidy and P. Shaver, pp. 3–22. New York, NY: Guilford Press.

Cath, S. (1965). Some dynamics of middle and later years: a study of depletion and restitution. In: *Geriatric Psychiatry: Grief, Loss, and Emotional Disorders in Aging Process*, eds. M. Berezin and S.H. Cath, pp. 21–72. New York, NY: International Universities Press.

Chapman, S. (2007). Immigration and its side effects. *Reason Magazine*, June 17, 2007.

Coates, L.B. and Fieldstone, C.A. (2008). Introduction: defining high conflict families. In: *Innovations in Interventions with High Conflict Families*, eds. L. Fieldstone and C. Coates, pp. 31–53. Madison, WI: Association of Family and Conciliation Courts.

Colarusso, C. (1997). Separation-individuation processes in middle adulthood: the fourth individuation. In: *The Seasons of Life: Separation-Individuation Perspectives*, eds. S. Akhtar and S. Kramer, pp. 73–94. Northvale, NJ: Aronson.

Colarusso, C. and Neimeroff, R. (1981). *Adult Development: A New Dimension in Psychodynamic Practice*. New York, NY: Plenum Press.

Colman, W. (1993). Marriage as a psychological container. In: *Psychotherapy with Couples: Theory and Practice at the Tavistock Institute of Marital Studies*, ed. S. Suszczynski, pp. 70–96. London, UK: Karnac Books.

Cristy, B.L. (2001). Wounded healer: the impact of a therapist's illness on the therapeutic situation. *Journal of the American Academy of Psychoanalysis* 29: 33–42.

Dasgupta, S.D. and Warrier, S. (1996). The footsteps of "Arundhati": Asian Indian women's experience of domestic violence in the United States. *Violence Against Women* 2: 238–259.

Davies, J.M. (2003). Falling in love with love. *Psychoanalytic Dialogues* 13: 1–27.

Diamond, D. (1992). Gender specific transference reactions of male and female patients to the therapist's pregnancy. *Psychoanalytic Psychology* 9: 319–345.

Diener, E., Gohm, C.L., Suh, E., and Oishi, S. (2000). Similarity of the relations between marital status and subjective well-being across cultures. *Journal of Cross-Cultural Psychology* 31: 419–436.

Duran-Aydintug, C. (1998). Emotional support during separation: its sources and determinants. *Journal of Divorce and Remarriage* 29: 121–141.

Ehrlich, J. (2014). *Divorce and Loss: Helping Adults and Children Mourn when a Marriage Comes Apart*. Lanham, MD: Rowman & Littlefield.

Eissler, K.R. (1993). On possible effects of aging on the practice of psychoanalysis. *Psychoanalytic Inquiry* 13: 316–332.

Emery, R.E. (1988). *Marriage, Divorce and Children's Adjustment*. Thousand Oaks, CA: Sage.

_____ (2013) *Cultural Sociology of Divorce: An Encyclopedia*. Thousand Oaks, CA: Sage.

Erikson, E. (1950). *Childhood and Society*. New York, NY: W.W. Norton.

_____ (1982). *The Life Cycle Completed: A Review*. New York, NY: W.W. Norton.

Evans, J.J. and Bloom, B.L. (1996). Effects of parental divorce among college under-graduates. *Journal of Divorce and Remarriage* 26: 69–91.

Fallon, A. and Brabender, V. (2003). *Awaiting the Therapist's Baby: A Guide for Parent-Practitioners*. New York, NY: Lawrence Erlbaum Associates.

Faulkner, W. (1951). *Requiem for a Nun*. New York, NY: Random House.

Feeney, B.C. and Monin, J.K. (2008). An attachment-theoretical perspective on divorce. In: *Handbook of Attachment: Theory, Research and Clinical Applications, Second Edition*, eds. J. Cassidy and P. Shaver, pp. 934–957. New York, NY: Guilford Press.

Finley, G.E. and Schwartz, S.J. (2010). The divided world of the child: Divorce and long-term psychosocial adjustment. *Family Court Review* 48: 516–527.

Fonagy, P. (2002). Developmental issues in normal adolescence and adolescent breakdown. In: *Affect Regulation, Mentalization, and the Development of the Self*, Chapter Eight, Electronic Edition. New York, NY: Other Press, 2005.

Fonagy, P., and Target, M. (2000). Playing with reality. *International Journal of Psychoanalysis* 81: 853–873.

_____ (2004). Playing with the reality of analytic love. *Psychoanalytic Dialogues* 14: 503–515.

Freud, S. (1895). Studies on hysteria. *Standard Edition* 2: 1–323.

_____ (1901). The psychopathology of everyday life. *Standard Edition* 6: 1–310.

_____ (1905). Three essays on the theory of sexuality. *Standard Edition* 7: 135–243.

_____ (1910). "Wild" psychoanalysis. *Standard Edition* 11: 219–228.

_____ (1914). On narcissism. *Standard Edition* 14:67–103.

_____ (1917a). Introductory lectures on psychoanalysis. *Standard Edition* 16.

_____ (1917b). Mourning and melancholia. *Standard Edition* 14: 237–260.

_____ (1930). Civilization and its discontents. *Standard Edition* 21: 64–145.

Friedman, G. (1991). Impact of a therapist's life-threatening illness on the therapeutic situation. *Contemporary Psychoanalysis* 27: 405–421.

Furtado, D., Macén, M., and Sevilla-Sanz, A. (2009). *Culture and Divorce: Evidence from European Immigrants to the US.* Presented at the European Association of Labour Economists Meeting, July 2009.

Furstenberg, F.F. Jr. and Cherlin, A. J. (1991). *Divided Families: What Happens to Children When Parents Part.* Cambridge, MA: Harvard University Press.

Gerstel, N. (1998). Divorce, gender, and social integration. *Gender and Society* 2: 343–367.

Gibbs, J. (1969). Marital status and suicide in the United States: a special test of status integration theory. *American Journal of Sociology* 74: 521–533.

Goldner, V. (2004). When love hurts. *Psychoanalytic Inquiry* 24: 346–372.

Gottman, J.M. (1994). *What Predicts Divorce? The Relationship Between Marital Processes and Marital Outcome.* Hillsdale, NJ: Erlbaum.

Gottman, J.M., Levenson, R.W., Swanson, C., Swanson, K., Tyson, R., and Yoshimoto, D. (2003). Observing gay, lesbian, and heterosexual couples' relationships: mathematical modeling of conflict interaction. *Journal of Homosexuality* 45: 65–91.

Gove, W.R. (1973). Sex, marital status, and mortality. *American Journal of Sociology* 79: 45–67.

Gove, W.R. and Shin, H. (1989). The psychological well-being of divorced and widowed men and women: an empirical analysis. *Journal of Family Issues* 10: 122–144.

Grinberg, L. and Grinberg, R. (1989). *Psychoanalytic Perspectives on Migration and Exile.* New Haven, CT: Yale University Press.

Gunsberg, L. (2016). Panel presentation on "The Effects of Divorce in Adults and Children." *Annual Meeting of the American Psychoanalytic Association*, January 16, 2016.

Gussow, M. (1998). A novelist builds out from fact to reach the truth. John Irving begins with his memories. *New York Times*, April 26, pp. E1, E3.

Guttman, S.A., Jones R.L., and Parrish, S.M., eds. (1980). *The Concordance to the Standard Edition of the Complete Psychological Works of Sigmund Freud.* Boston, MA: G.K. Hall.

Healy, J.M., Stewart, A.J., and Copeland, A.P. (1993). The role of self-blame in children's adjustment to parental separation. *Personality and Social Psychology Bulletin* 19: 279–289.

Herek, G.M. (2006). Legal recognition of same-sex relationships in the United States: a social science perspective. *American Psychologist* 61: 607–621.

Hetherington, E.M. and Camara, K.A. (1984). Families in transition: the process of dissolution and reconstitution. In: *Review of Child Development: Vol. 7. The Family,* ed. R.D. Parke, pp. 398–440. Chicago, IL: University of Chicago Press.

Hetherington, E.M., Cox, M., and Cox, R. (1978). The aftermath of divorce. In: *Mother-Child, Father-Child Relationships*, eds. J.H. Stevens, Jr. and M. Matthews, pp. 149–176. Washington, DC: National Association for the Education of Young Children.

_____ (1982). The effects of divorce on parents and children. In: *Nontraditional Families*, ed. M. Lamb, pp. 233–288. Hillsdale, NJ: Erlbaum.

Hetherington, E.M. and Kelly, J. (2002). *For Better or for Worse: Divorce Reconsidered*. New York, NY: W.W. Norton.

Hetherington, M. and Stanley-Hagan, M. (1999). The adjustment of children with divorced parents. *Journal of Child Psychology and Psychiatry* 40: 129–140.

Hodges, W.F. (1991). *Interventions for Children of Divorce: Custody, Access, and Psychotherapy* (2nd ed). Hoboken, New Jersey: John Wiley and Sons, Inc.

Irving, J. (1976). *The World According to Garp*. New York, NY: Ballentine/Random.

_____ (1997). *The Cider House Rules*. New York, NY: Ballentine/Random.

_____ (1998). *A Widow for One Year*. New York, NY: Ballentine/Random.

Jacobson, E. (1965). The return of the lost parent. In: *Drives, Affects, Behavior, Vol. 2*, ed. M. Schur, pp. 193–211. New York, NY: International Universities Press.

Johnson, C.L. (1988). Active and latent functions of grandparenting during the divorce process. *The Gerontologist* 28: 185–191.

Johnson, C.L., and Barer, B. (1987). Marital instability and the changing kinship networks of grandparents. *The Gerontologist* 27: 330–335.

Johnson, H. (2015). *Unique Iceland*. Icelandic Airways Documentary.

Johnston, J.R. and Campbell, L.E.G. (1988). *Impasses of Divorce: The Dynamics and Resolution of Family Conflict*. New York: The Free Press.

Johnston, J.R., Roseby, V., and Kuehnle, K. (2009). *In the name of the child: A developmentalapproach to understanding and helping children of conflicted and violent divorce* (Second Edition). New York: Springer Publishing Company.

Joung, I.M.A., Stronks, K., van der Mheen, H., van Poppel, F.W.A., van der Meer, J.B.W., and Mackenbach, J.P. (1997). The contribution of intermediary factors to marital status differences in self-reported health. *Journal of Marriage and the Family* 59: 476–490.

Kalmijn, M. (1993). Spouse selection among the children of European immigrants: a comparison of marriage cohorts in the 1960 Census. *International Migration Review* 727: 51–78.

Kalter, N. (1990). *Growing up with Dvorce: Helping Your Child Avoid Immediate and Later Emotional Problems*. New York, NY: Free Press.

Kaplan, E.H., Weiss, S., Harris, L., and Dick, M. (1994). Termination imposed by the analyst's relocation: theoretical and practical considerations. *Canadian Journal of Psychoanalysis* 2: 253–267.

Kaslow, F. (1991). The sociocultural context of divorce. *Contemporary Family Therapy* 13: 583–607.

Kavaler-Adler, S. (2007). Pivotal moments of surrender to mourning the internal parental object. *Psychoanalytic Review* 94: 763–789.

Kennedy, G.E. (1989). College students' relationship with grandparents. *Psychological Reports* 64: 477–478.

Khoo, S-E. and Zhao, Z. (2001). A decomposition of immigrant divorce rates in Australia. *Journal of Population Research* 18: 68–77.

Kirshner, L. (2012). Towards an ethics of psychoanalysis: a critical reading of Lacan's ethics. *Journal of the American Psychoanalytic Association* 60:1223–1242.

Kitson, G.C. (1982). Attachment to the spouse in divorce: a scale and its application. *Journal of Marriage and the Family* 44: 379–393.

Kitson, G.C. and Morgan, L.A. (1990). The multiple consequences of divorce: A decade review. *Journal of Marriage and the Family* 52: 913–924.

Kivnick, H.Q. (1982). Grandparenthood: An overview of meaning and mental health. *The Gerontologist* 22: 59–66.

Klein, M. (1940). Mourning and its relation to manic-depressive states. In: *Love, Guilt, and Reparation and Other Works, 1921–1945*, pp. 344–369. New York, NY: Free Press, 1975.

Kogan, I. (2007). *The Struggle Against Mourning*. Lanham, MD: Jason Aronson.

Kornhaber, A. and Woodward, K. L. (1981). *Grandparents/Grandchildren: The Vital Connection*. Garden City, NJ: Anchor Press/Doubleday.

Kranjac, D. (2016). Intergenerational transmission of stress vulnerability and resilience following trauma: extreme trauma affects FKBP5 methylation in survivors of the Holocaust as well as in their offspring. *Psychiatry Advisor*, May 26, 2016.

Kurdek, L.A. (1995). Lesbian and gay couples. In: *Lesbian, Gay and Bisexual Identities over the Lifespan*, eds. A.R. D'Augelli and C.J. Patterson, pp. 243–261. New York, NY: Oxford University Press.

Kurdek, L.A. (1997). Adjustment to relationship dissolution in gay, lesbian and heterosexual partners. *Personal Relationships* 4: 145–161.

Kurdek, L.A. (2004). Are gay and lesbian cohabitating couples really different from heterosexual married couples? *Journal of Marriage and Family* 66: 880–900.

Kurdek, L.A. (2005). What do we know about gay and lesbian couples? *American Psychological Society* 14: 251–254.

Lang, F.R., Staudinger, U.M., and Cartensen, L.L. (1998). Perspectives on socioemotional selectivity in late life: how personality and social context do (and do not) make a difference. *Journals of Gerontology* 53B: 21–30.

Larner, M. (1990). Local residential mobility and its effects on social networks: a cross-cultural comparison. In: *Extending Families: The Social Networks of Parents and Their Children*, eds. M. Cochran, M. Larner, D. Riley, L. Gunnarsson, and C.R. Henderson, Jr., pp. 205–229. Cambridge, UK: Cambridge University Press.

Lawlor, D. (2012). Commentary on chapter ten. In: *How Couple Relationships Shape our World: Clinical practice, Research, and Policy Perspectives*, eds. A. Balfour, M. Morgan, and C. Vincent, pp. 297–305. London, UK: Karnac Books.

Lear, J. (2000). Introduction. In *The Essential Loewald: Collected Papers and Monographs* (pp. xi–xl). Hagerstown, Maryland: University Publishing Group.

Leonoff, A. (2015). *The Good Divorce: A Psychoanalyst's Exploration of Separation, Divorce, and Children*. London, UK: Karnac Books.

Levinson, D., Darrow, C., Klein, E., Levinson, M., and McKee, B. (1978). *The Seasons of a Man's Life*. New York, NY: Alfred Knopf.

Lillard, L.A. and Waite, L.J. (1995). 'Til death do us part: marital disruption and mortality. *American Journal of Sociology* 100: 1131–1156.

Loewald, H. (1977). The waning of the Oedipus complex. In: *Papers on Psychoanalysis*. New Haven, CT: Yale University Press, 1980.

Loewald, H. (2000). On the therapeutic action of psychoanalysis. In: *The Essential Loewald: Collected Papers and Monographs*, pp. 221–256. Hagerstown, MD: University Publishing Group.

Lohr, R.B., Chethik, M., Press, S.E., and Solyom, A.E. (1981). Impact of divorce on children: vicissitudes and therapeutic implications of the reconciliation fantasy. *Journal of Child Psychotherapy* 7: 123–136.

Macoby, E.E. and Mnookin, R.H. (1992). *Dividing the Child: Social and Legal Dilemmas of Custody*. Cambridge, MA: Harvard University Press.

Madden-Derdich, D.A. and Arditti, J.A. (1999). The ties that bind: attachment between former spouses. *Family Relations* 48: 243–249.

Magdol, L. (2000). The people you know: the impact of residential mobility on mothers' social network ties. *Journal of Social and Personal Relationships* 17: 183–204.

Marquardt, E. (2005). *Between Two Worlds: The Inner Lives of Children of Divorce*. New York, NY: Three Rivers Press.

Masheter, C. (1990). Postdivorce relationships between exspouses: a literature review. *Journal of Divorce and Remarriage* 14: 97–122.

Masheter, C. (1991). Postdivorce relationships between ex-spouses: the roles of attachment and interpersonal conflict. *Journal of Marriage and the Family* 53: 103–110.

McEwan, I. (1997). *Enduring Love*. New York, NY: Anchor Books.

Mikulincer, M. and Florian, V. (1996). Emotional reactions to interpersonal losses over the life span: an attachment theoretical perspective. In: *Handbook of Emotions, Adult Development, and Aging*, eds. C. Magai and S.H. McFadden, pp. 269–285. San Diego, CA: Academic Press.

Miller, J.G. (1994). Cultural diversity in the morality of caring: individually-oriented versus duty-based interpersonal moral codes. *Cross-Cultural Research* 28: 3–39.

Miller, J.G. and Bersoff, D.M. (1992). Culture and moral judgment: how are conflicts between justice and friendship resolved? *Journal of Personality and Social Psychology* 62: 541–554.

Miller, J.G., Bersoff, D.M., and Harwood, R.L. (1990). Perceptions of social responsibilities in India and in the United States: moral imperatives or personal decision? *Journal of Personality and Social Psychology* 58: 33–47.

Miller, J.G. and Luthar, S. (1989). Issues of interpersonal responsibility and accountability: a comparison of Indians' and Americans' moral judgments. *Social Cognition* 3: 237–261.

Miller, N.B., Smerglia, V.L., Gaudet, D.S., and Kitons, G.C. (1998). Stressful life events, social support, and the distress of widowed and divorced women. *Journal of Family Issues* 19: 181–203.

Mirowsky, J. and Ross, C.E. (2003). *Education, Social Status, and Health.* Hawthorne, NY: Aldine de Gruyter.

Mohr, J. (2008). Same-sex romantic attachment. In: *Handbook of Attachment: Theory, Research and Clinical Applications, Second Edition*, eds. J. Cassidy and P. Shaver, pp. 482–502. New York, NY: Guilford Press.

Moore, G. (1990). Structural determinants of men's and women's personal networks. *American Sociological Review* 55: 726–735.

Morgan, D., Carder, P., and Neal, M. (1997). Are some relationships more useful than others? The value of similar others in the networks of recent widows. *Journal of Social and Personal Relationships* 14: 745–760.

Morgan, M. (2005). On being able to be a couple: the importance of a "creative couple" in psychic life. In: *Oedipus and the Couple*, ed. F. Grier, pp. 9–30. London, UK: Karnac Books.

Morgan, M. (2012). How couple therapists work with parenting issues. In: *How Couple Relationships Shape our World: Clinical practice, Research, and Policy Perspectives*, eds. A. Balfour, M. Morgan, and C. Vincent, pp. 71–83. London, UK: Karnac Books.

Offer, D. and Sabshin, M. (1966). *Normality: Theoretical and Clinical Concepts of Mental Health.* New York, NY: Basic Books.

Olinick, S. (1976). Parallel analyzing functions in work ego and observing ego. *Journal of the Philadelphia Association for Psychoanalysis* 3: 3–21.

Page, T. and Bretherton, I. (2001). Mother- and father-child attachment themes in the story completions of pre-schoolers from post-divorce families: do they predict relationships with peers and teachers? *Attachment and Human Development* 3: 1–29.

_____ (2003). Representations of attachment to father in the narratives of pre-school girls in post-divorce families: implications for family relationships and social development. *Child and Adolescent Social Work Journal* 20: 99–122.

Parens, H. (2008) A self-study of resilience: healing from the Holocaust. In: *The Unbroken Soul: Tragedy, Trauma and Human Resilience*, eds. H. Parens, H.P. Blum and S. Akhtar, pp. 87–116. Lanham, MD: Rowman & Littlefield.

Peplau, L.A. and Spalding, L.R. (2000). The close relationships of lesbians, gay men and bisexuals. In: *Close Relationships: A Sourcebook*, eds. C. Hendrick and S.S. Hendrick, pp. 111–123. Thousand Oaks, CA: Sage.

Peters, A. and Liefbroer, A.C. (1997). Beyond marital status: partner history and well-being in old age. *Journal of Marriage and the Family* 59: 687–699.

Pew Research Center (2014). Millennials in adulthood: detached from institutions, networked with friends. *Social and Demographic Trends*, March 7, 2014.

Piemont, L. (2009) The epigenesis of psychopathology in children of divorce. *Modern Psychoanalysis* 34: 98–116.

Prall, R.C. (2000). *The Rights of Children in Separation and Divorce: The Essential Handbook for Parents.* Kansas City, MO: Landmark.

Prathikanti, S. (1997). East Indian American families. In: *Working with Asian Americans: A Guide to Clinicians*, ed. E. Lee, pp. 79–100. New York, NY: Guilford Press.

Rands, M. (1988). Changes in social networks following marital separation and divorce. In: *Families and Social Networks*, ed. R.M. Milardo, pp. 127–146. Newbury Park, CA: Sage.

Reibstein, J. (1998). Attachment, pain, and detachment for the adults in divorce. *Sexual and Marital Therapy* 13: 351–360.

Roch, L. and Roch, V. (2010). www.divorcesaloon.com/2010/12/16/divorce-custody-in-new-york-divorce-custody-in-iceland-a-comparative-study. Accessed March 31, 2016.

Rosbrow-Reich, S. (1988). Identity and growth: a psychoanalytic study of divorce. *Psychoanalytic Review* 75: 419–441.

Ross, J.M. (1994). *What Men Want*. Cambridge, MA: Harvard University Press.

Ruszczynski, S. (1995). Introduction. *Intrusiveness and Intimacy in the Couple*. London, UK: Karnac Books.

_____ (2005). Reflective space in the intimate couple relationship: the "marital triangle." In: *Oedipus and the Couple*, ed. F. Grier, pp. 31–47. London, UK: Karnac Books.

Samera, T. and Stolberg, A.L. (1993). Peer support, divorce, and children's adjustment. *Journal of Divorce and Remarriage* 20: 45–64.

Sandler, I.N., Tein, J.Y., and West, S.G. (1994). Coping, stress, and the psychological symptoms of children of divorce: a cross sectional and longitudinal study. *Child Development* 65: 1744–1763.

Sbarra, D.A. and Emery, R.E. (2005). The emotional sequelae of non-marital relationship dissolution: analysis of change and intra-individual variability over time. *Personal Relationships* 12: 213–232.

Schlachet, P. (1996). When the therapist divorces. In: *The Therapist as a Person*, ed. B. Gerson, pp. 141–157. Hillsdale, NJ: Analytic Press.

Schlesinger, H. (2001). Technical problems in analyzing the mourning patient. In: *Three Faces of Mourning*, ed. S. Akhtar, pp. 115–39. Northvale, NJ: Jason Aronson.

Schole, R. and Phataralaoha, A. (2000). *Mail-Order Bride Industry and its Impact on US Immigration*. http://www.wwdl.net/information/immigration, accessed March 5, 2016.

Schwartz, H. and Silver, A-L. (1990). *Illness in the Analyst: Implications for the Treatment Relationship*. Madison, CT: International Universities Press.

Shane, E. (2002). The transformative effects of separation and divorce on analytic treatment. *Psychoanalytic Inquiry* 22: 580–598.

Silitsky, D. (1996). Correlates of psychosocial adjustment in adolescents from divorced families. *Journal of Divorce and Remarriage* 26: 151–169.

Silverman, M.A. (2001). Stepdaughters and stepfathers: living together in a haunted house. In: *Stepparenting: Creating and Recreating Families in America Today*, eds. S.H. Cath and M. Shopper, pp. 147–164. Hillsdale, NJ: Analytic Press.

Smerglia, V.L., Miller, N.B., and Kort-Butler, L. (1999). The impact of social support on women's adjustment to divorce: a literature review and analysis. *Journal of Divorce and Remarriage* 32: 63–89.

Solomon, J. and George, C. (1999). The development of attachment in separated and divorced families: the effects of overnight visitation, parent and couple variables. *Attachment and Human Development* 1: 2–33.

Solomon, S.E., Rothblum, E.D., and Balsam, K.F. (2005). Money, housework, sex and conflict: same-sex couples in civil unions, those not in civil unions, and heterosexual married siblings. *Sex Roles* 52: 561–575.

Southwick, S.M., Ozbay, F., and Mayes, L.C. (2008). Psychological and biological factors associated with resilience to stress and trauma. In: *The Unbroken Soul: Tragedy, Trauma and Human Resilience*, eds. H. Parens, H.P. Blum and S. Akhtar, pp. 129–151. Lanham, MD: Rowman & Littlefield.

Stack, S. (1980). Domestic integration and the rate of suicide: a comparative study. *Journal of Comparative Family Studies* 11: 249–260.

Stack, S. (1990). The impact of divorce on suicide: new micro level data. *Journal of Marriage and the Family* 52: 119–127.

Stolle, D.P., Wexler, D.B., and Winick, B.J., eds. (2000). *Practicing Therapeutic Jurisprudence: Law as a Helping Profession*. Durham, NC: Carolina Academic Press.

Stuart, J.J. (1997). Pregnancy in the therapist: consequences of a gradually discernible physical change. *Psychoanalytic Psychology* 14: 347–364.

Sullivan, H. (1953). *The Interpersonal Theory of Psychiatry*, eds. H.S. Perry and M.L. Gawel. New York, NY: W.W. Norton.

Sung, B.L. (1990). Chinese American intermarriage. *Journal of Comparative Family Studies* 21: 337–352.

Tallmer, M. (1992). The aging analyst. *Psychoanalytic Review* 79: 381–404.

Teja, S. and Stolberg, A.L. (1993). Peer support, divorce and children's adjustment. *Journal of Divorce and Remarriage* 20: 45–64.

Terhell, E.L., Broese van Groenou, M.I., and Van Tilburg, T. (2004). Network dynamics in the long-term period after divorce. *Journal of Social and Personal Relationships* 21: 719–738.

Tessman, L.H. (1996). *Helping Children Cope with Parting Parents*. Northvale, NJ: Jason Aronson.

Thuen, F. and Eikeland, O.J. (1998). Social support among males and females after marital disruption. *Psychology, Health and Medicine* 3: 315–326.

Triandis, H.C., Bontempo, R., Villareal, M.J., Asai, M., and Lucca, N. (1988). Individualism and collectivism: cross-cultural perspectives on self in group relationships. *Journal of Personality and Social Psychology* 34: 323–338.

Umberson, D. (1987). Family status and health behaviors: social control as a dimension of social integration. *Journal of Health and Social Behavior* 28: 306–319.

Umberson, D., Chen, M.D., House, J.S., Hopkins, K., and Slaten, E. (1996). The effect of social relationships on psychological well-being: are men and women really so different? *American Sociological Review* 61: 837–857.

United Nations Human Development Index in Human Development Report (2015). New York, NY: United Nations Development Programme.

United States Census Bureau Report (2011). Washington DC: Census Bureau Publications.

United States Census Bureau Report (2015). Washington DC: Census Bureau Publications.

Vaillant, G. (1977). *Adaptation to Life*. Boston, MA: Little, Brown.

Verbrugge, L.M. (1979). Marital status and health. *Journal of Marriage and Family* 41: 267–285.

Walcott, D. (1992). Nobel lecture: The Antilles: Fragments of epic memory. http://www.nobelprize.org/nobel_prizes/literature/laureates/1992/walcott-lecture.html. Retrieved June 4, 2016.

Wallerstein, J. (1990). Transference and countertransference in clinical interventions with divorcing families. *American Journal of Orthopsychiatry* 60: 337–345.

Wallerstein, J. and Blakeslee, S. (1989). *Second Chances: Men, Women, and Children a Decade after Divorce*. New York, NY: Houghton Mifflin, 2004.

_____ (2003). *What About the Kids? Raising Your Children Before, During, and After Divorce*. New York, NY: Hyperion.

Wallerstein, J., and Kelly, J. (1980). *Surviving the Breakup: How Children and Parents Cope with Divorce*. New York, NY: Basic Books.

Wallerstein, J., Lewis, J.M., and Blakeslee, S. (2000). *The Unexpected Legacy of Divorce: A 25 Year Landmark Study*. New York, NY: Hyperion.

Whitaker, C.A. and Miller, M.H. (1969). A reevaluation of psychiatric help when divorce impends. *American Journal of Psychiatry* 126: 57–64.

Weiss, R.S. (1975). *Marital Separation*. New York, NY: Basic Books.

Weiss, R.S. (1976). The emotional impact of marital separation. *Journal of Social Issues* 32: 135–145.

Winnicott, D.W. (1956). *Through Paediatrics to Psychoanalysis: Collected Papers*. New York, NY: Basic Books.

_____ (1960). Ego distortion in terms of true and false self. In: *Maturational Processes and the Facilitating Environment*, pp. 140–152. New York, NY: International Universities Press, 1965.

_____ (1965). *The Maturational Processes and the Facilitating Environment*. New York, NY: International Universities Press.

Wolf-Amansreh (1991). Mein Partner oder Partnerin kommt aus einem anderen Land. Inter-kulturelle Ehen, Familien und Parnerschaften. *Ein Wegweiser für die Selbsthilfe, IAF, Verband bi-nationaler Familien und Partnerschaften.* Frankfurt, Germany: Interessengemeinschaft der mit Ausländern verheirateten Frauen e.V.

Index

About the Editor and Contributors

Salman Akhtar, MD, Professor of Psychiatry, Sidney Kimmel Medical College, Thomas Jefferson University, Training and Supervising Analyst, Psychoanalytic Center of Philadelphia, Philadelphia, PA.

Stephen J. Anderer, PhD, JD, Founder and Partner, Momjian Anderer LLC, Philadelphia, PA.

Suzanne Benser, MD, Faculty member, Psychoanalytic Center of Philadelphia, Philadelphia, PA.

Shawn Blue, PhD, Assistant Professor, Sidney Kimmel Medical College; Psychologist, Student Personal Counseling Center, Department of Psychiatry and Human Behavior, The Thomas Jefferson University, Philadelphia, PA.

Joshua Ehrlich, PhD, Faculty, Michigan Psychoanalytic Institute; Adjunct Faculty, Department of Psychiatry, University of Michigan School of Medicine, Ann Arbor, MI.

Corinne Masur, PsyD, Faculty member, Psychoanalytic Center of Philadelphia, Philadelphia, PA.

Kathleen Ross, PhD, LCSW, Faculty member, Psychoanalytic Center of Philadelphia, Philadelphia, PA.

Martin A. Silverman, MD, Training and Supervising Analyst, and Supervising Child Analyst, Institute for Psychoanalytic Education NYU

School of Medicine, Associate Editor and Book Review Editor, *Psychoanalytic Quarterly*; Private practice, Maplewood, NJ.

Elizabeth H. Thomas, MTS, MSW, PhD, Faculty, New Directions Program of the Washington Center for Psychoanalysis; Private practice, Chevy Chase, MD.

CPSIA information can be obtained
at www.ICGtesting.com
Printed in the USA
BVOW08s0024011216
469368BV00001B/3/P

9 781442 279322